FAITH FOR
THE TIMES

By Alan Redpath:

VICTORIOUS CHRISTIAN LIVING
VICTORIOUS PRAYING
VICTORIOUS CHRISTIAN SERVICE
THE ROYAL ROUTE TO HEAVEN
THE MAKING OF A MAN OF GOD
BLESSINGS OUT OF BUFFETINGS
FAITH FOR THE TIMES Part One
FAITH FOR THE TIMES Part Two

FAITH FOR THE TIMES

Studies in the Prophecy of Isaiah
Chapters 49 to 54

Part II THE PLAN OF
DELIVERANCE

ALAN REDPATH

LONDON
PICKERING & INGLIS LTD

Scripture references in this volume are from the King James Version of the Bible.

The excerpt from K.A.M. Kelly's hymn, "Give Me a Sight O Saviour," Copyright National Young Life Campaign, Great Britain. Used by permission.

Excerpt from the hymn "I Cannot Tell" by W. Y. Fullerton by courtesy of the Psalms & Hymns Trust, London, England.

Excerpt from the hymn "O Breath of Life" by Mrs. Bessie Porter Head is used by permission.

Excerpts from the two hymns, "Love, Wonderful Love," and "Give Me a Heart Like Thine," are from the Keswick Hymnbook published by the Scripture Union, London, England.

Copyright © 1974 by Fleming H. Revell Company

First Pickering & Inglis printing 1975

ISBN 0 7208 0354 3
Cat. No. 01/0617

*Printed in Great Britain by
Lowe & Brydone (Printers) Ltd, Thetford, Norfolk*

Contents

Preface

This second part of *Faith for the Times* touches on some of the most wonderful portions of the Word of God. These have been ably expounded by many great men whose shoes I am not worthy to unloose. I have sought with the help of the Lord to put into print simply and clearly some basic things which these chapters in Isaiah proclaim. My hope is that pastors, Sunday-school teachers, and Bible-study-group leaders in homes and churches may find some helpful thoughts in them.

At the time these messages were preached, the Lord graciously used them to bring people to a saving knowledge of Christ, and Christians into a deeper walk with Him. That the printed page may accomplish just that is my earnest prayer.

ALAN REDPATH

FAITH FOR THE TIMES

1

Isaiah 49:8-11, 14-16

The Love That Never Gives Up

Thus saith the Lord, In an acceptable time have I heard thee, and in a day of salvation have I helped thee: and I will preserve thee, and give thee for a covenant of the people, to establish the earth, to cause to inherit the desolate heritages; That thou mayest say to the prisoners, Go forth; to them that are in darkness, Shew yourselves. They shall feed in the ways, and their pastures shall be in all high places. They shall not hunger nor thirst; neither shall the heat nor sun smite them: for he that hath mercy on them shall lead them, even by the springs of water shall he guide them. And I will make all my mountains a way, and my highways shall be exalted. . . . But Zion said, The Lord hath forsaken me, and my Lord hath forgotten me. Can a woman forget her sucking child, that she should not have compassion on the son of her womb? yea, they may forget, yet will I not forget thee. Behold, I have graven thee upon the palms of my hands; thy walls are continually before me.

Isaiah 49: 8-11, 14-16

This chapter is full of our Lord Jesus Christ, and the words quoted could not possibly have their complete fulfillment in any other save in our Saviour.

Isaiah 49, however, is spoken primarily to the Jews. Now if you ask me how it can be spoken to the Israelites and about our Lord Jesus at the same time, I would just remind you that when they for the second time failed in the purpose of their captivity and returned from Babylon, they ultimately became religiously

11

a race of Pharisees and legalists without love or compassion for others. The Lord Jesus took over the responsibilities they evaded; He fulfilled the purpose which they failed to fulfill by the gospel He taught and by the church He formed. In the mission of Jesus Christ, the heart of Judaism unfolded itself. He was the perfect fulfillment of all they had failed to be.

But this is not only a chapter which has to do with our Lord and the Jews. For the purpose of our study it has to do with the hearts and lives of men and women in the world today. I want, therefore, to maintain the consistency of thought in this second part of Isaiah, and consider this passage in relation to its message to our own personal life.

First, fasten your attention on verse 16 of this chapter, where our Lord says, "Behold, I have graven thee upon the palms of my hands; thy walls are continually before me." These words in their context are the answer of God to His people's complaint that He had forgotten them! "But Zion said, The Lord hath forsaken me, and my Lord hath forgotten me" (v.14). Humanly speaking, of course, they had every reason to think that would be so, for this chapter anticipates a time when they had languished for nearly seventy years in the bondage and captivity of Babylon and had been crushed and overwhelmed by the power of that great empire. Between them and home, hope, and joy in Jerusalem were deserts, mountains, apparently unsurmountable objects, and they seemed to be completely trapped. In any case, they had only bitter memories of a home that lay in ruins, for Jerusalem lay in waste, a mass of debris. You recall that when Nehemiah visited the scene a few years later, so terrible was the destruction of the city that the animal upon which he rode could not pass over it. So hopeless did the situation seem that his determination to rebuild the wall was scorned. Oh yes, there was many a reason for His people to say, "The Lord hath forsaken us."

Whenever we look at God through circumstances, we are inclined to think like that. But when God enables us to look at circumstances through Him, then we think differently; this is exactly what the Lord seeks to do in this tremendous passage of Scripture. How can I, He says, bring this people to a new hope, to a new confidence, to a new courage, to a new step of faith, to a new obedience, to a new commitment? How can I bring them to see that there is a way through from their captivity? It can only be if they understand the depth of My love.

So the Lord brings to them, through His prophet, the assurance of a love that cannot fail, that will never let go, and He says to them, "I have graven thee upon the palms of my hands; thy walls are continually before me."

I am thinking of some readers who may feel as those people felt: "God has forgotten and forsaken me." Perhaps you are comfortless, or sorrowing, or afflicted. Even worse than that, as a Christian you think you have grieved the Holy Spirit so seriously that you feel yourself beyond any possibility of recovery. Life is so full of obstacles and difficulties and impossible contradictions, it seems at times the tangles can never be straightened out. You have often attempted to do so but just as often you have failed, and indeed it seems you are doomed to failure.

What is God's message to such a heart? He has no new plan, but I believe He does want you to understand, as you have never understood before, the meaning of His love. As I seek to open up this passage, I pray the Spirit of God may talk to you at depth about the love of Jesus. In the first place, when God says, "I will make all my mountains a way. . . ." that leads me to suggest to you that the love of God is *invincible in its purpose.* Though there be great mountains and unsurpassable obstacles between Babylon and Jerusalem, what does God do about them? He won't remove them, but He will make the mountains—which seem to these people to be insurmountable obstacles—actually to contribute to their deliverance.

Each of us has some mountain in our lives somewhere, something that threatens to bar spiritual progress, and frustrate every hope, something that creates a sense of failure and collapse, a daily cross, a thorn in the flesh, a sin. "Oh, if only these were removed," you say, "how much holier a life I could live! How much more satisfactory a Christian I could be!" Having said that, you pray, "Lord, give me patience, and please remove this awful thing that tests me beyond endurance." Yes, you have supposed that the obstacle which you try to avoid and escape from is the biggest hindrance in your life. If only it would go, how patient you would be.

On the contrary, if it went, the temptation to be impatient would have been removed and that would not help to make you patient. Patience only comes through facing the trial *that God puts there*, for His Word tells us that "tribulation worketh patience" (Romans 5:3). Sometimes the troubles that I try to avoid —the situation from which I try to escape and the circumstances which I drive away from me—are the very things in the hand of God which sanctify me and make me like the Lord Jesus. That which I dread is often the instrument God uses to make His mountains a way.

You notice He says: "I will make all my mountains a way. . . ." There is no exception in that great, but little word, *all.* There is nothing in life—no obstacle, no loneliness, no trial, no sorrow—which may not be a way into God's richest blessing. There is no situation of entanglement, nothing that you can possibly conceive, but this can be part of God's way to make His mountain a way of deliverance.

Then notice the pronoun, "I will make *my* mountains." Yes, they are His. He put them there, He will make them a way. If I can see only a mountain filling my whole horizon, when I reach its foot I will discover there is a path.

What is the secret, therefore, of discovering that the love of God is invincible in its purpose? It's just this, the commitment of your life to Jesus Christ without reservation, then you can go to meet your mountains and meet obstacles in Jesus—not to meet them outside Him, but in Christ. If you do that, then the mountain between you and God's land of blessing becomes the way into it.

Do I speak to someone whose life appears to be confronted with nothing but mountains that seem to be in front of you and on all sides? You face them and you almost despair.

Friend, have you ever taken a moment to look back and to reflect on the past? What did you find there? You found surrounding you nothing but mountains that seemed to be absolutely insurmountable. Look back a moment at those mountains. Not one, but every mountain that you have ever confronted was levelled out flat by the Lord, and as you look back you see that everything is a plain. Yet in front of you everywhere there are still more mountains! Surely the God who has removed every mountain thus far will remove the one that confronts you right now. Face it therefore, face that mountain, that obstacle, that impossibility, whatever it is, face it in Jesus and watch Him make it a way. The love of God is invincible in its purpose.

Now look at verse 15 of this chapter, and let me suggest to you that the love of God is absolutely *impassable in its preciousness:* "Can a woman forget her . . . child? . . . yea, they may forget, yet will I not forget thee."

Here, to encourage a despondent people to believe, the Holy Spirit uses the illustration of a mother's love as she bends over her little child. Perhaps she soothes it in times of suffering; she may even watch the little life flickering out. At all times she is there constantly, ready to surrender food, sleep, anything, for the sake of that little one. A mother's love follows us all through life, though often we don't understand it, but resent and rebel against it. Is there any love that quite replaces the love of a mother? She is the one who prays for her child from infancy, and at the first signs of distress she is there. Her love would stand by him even if one day he became a prisoner in the dock.

The Holy Spirit teaches that the love of a mother is but a dim reflection of the love of God. There is much more than a mother's love in the love of Jesus. She, says the Scripture, may forget; He never can. We may fall so far down and get in such an appalling mess that our dearest and nearest forget and forsake. We may have been so far away from God that perhaps someone who put a candle in his window, hoping we would come back, has given up hope. Maybe the fire of love in the hearts of those near and dear to you has died down until nobody cares. But my Bible says, "When my father and my mother forsake me, then the Lord will take me up" (Psalm 27:10), because "I have loved thee with an everlasting love" (Jeremiah 31:3). It tells me that the Lord Jesus loved His disciples and having loved His own, He loved them unto the end. His is a love that is absolutely impassable in its preciousness, that never gives up and never lets go. To the person who feels utterly bereft and forsaken by God, I can but point you to that love and ask you (though you may never entirely understand it) to believe in it, to rest in it, and to rejoice in it even now. There is a children's chorus that presents a wonderful truth:

Love, wonderful love, the love of God to me!
Love, wonderful love, so great, so rich, so free!
Wide, wide as the ocean; deep, deep as the sea;
High, as high as the heavens above, His love to me!

Dare I believe that today? Dare you?

I find something else about the love of God which is even more amazing. Look for a moment at our text which states that the love of God is absolutely *indelible in its penetration.* "I have graven thee upon the palms of my hands; thy walls are continually before me." The hand of God—the hand of power, the hand of authority, the hand by which He upholds all things by His strength, but more than this, the hand of love—the hand of God. One day the Lord Jesus stepped into a room when He had risen from the dead and He showed His disciples His hands and His side. "I have graven thee upon the palms of my hands. . . ." He does not say, "I have tattooed thee," for a tattoo mark could come off, but "I have graven thee." He shows us His hands, and that with which our names are graven there was a sword and a spear and a nail, that drove holes into His hands, His feet, and His side. "I have graven thee upon the palms of my hands."

Never are you out of the sight of God, never out of His thoughts, your very lives are photographed in a place where God always sees them. He could never forget them. They can never be obliterated. In the Book of Revelation, John is given a vision of glory and he says, "I beheld . . . in the midst of the throne . . . a Lamb as it had been slain" (Revelation 5:6). Throughout all eternity there is One from whom the marks of suffering are never removed and who is the constant source of joy of all in the glory, who cry, ". . . worthy art thou, for thou hast redeemed us to God by thy blood" (*see* Revelation 5:9). This surely is a demonstration of a love that is absolutely indelible in its penetration.

To some person who feels so utterly and completely hopeless I ask you not to look at *things* and then try to look at God, but to look at the throne in eternity and the nail-pierced hands of Jesus, for that is where God has put you.

Look at what the verse goes on to say: ". . . thy walls are

continually before me." From the point of view of the people in Isaiah's day, all they could see was ruin, destruction, debris; their memory was of a city that was flattened out, whose walls had been destroyed and all lay in ruins. But God speaks to them at this moment of their captivity: ". . . thy walls [not your ruins —not your past failure, your breakdown, your sin—but your walls, the thing that I purposed for you, that which I intended you to be] are continually before me."

If someone feels in his heart the situation is hopeless, I say you are looking at the ruins of life, while God looks at the walls. You look at what you have been and you are conscious of awful failure; but bless the Lord, He sees you in Christ, as what He intends you to be. He sees you as what you long to be in your best moments. He sees you as what you will be when the grace of God has finished the task.

We look back on failure and frustration, disappointment and breakdown, but I bid you today to look beyond all this, to look off to the Lord Jesus, for I read in His Word, "I saw a new Jerusalem, descending out of heaven from God, having the glory of God, adorned as a bride for her husband" (*see* Revelation 21:2). That is the ultimate purpose in His heart, for all His people. Your names are graven on the palms of His hands; and your walls are *continually* before Him.

How good to know in my heart today that God looks at me in Jesus Christ! He does not see that which is gone, for it is all buried in the depths of the sea. He sees me as He intends to make me. Nothing can destroy His purpose; the task is complete and He sees *me* complete in the Lord Jesus—a love that is absolutely indelible in its penetration.

As we look further into this chapter we see a love that is *infinite in its powerfulness*. Look at verse 24; I find here the language of someone who is disconsolate, who feels the hopelessness of the situation as he says: "Shall the prey be taken from the mighty, or the lawful captive delivered?"

Israel has become a helpless captive in the heart of a mighty empire, and perhaps today in your soul you are a helpless captive to the devil. In your weakness and impotency you try to break through and make your exodus, but no sooner had you started than you broke down and you are back again, and the cry is wrung from your soul, "I'm just a captive" and "Shall the prey be taken from the mighty, or the lawful captive delivered?" How can it ever be? The Lord God has calculated His resources. Never let the difficulties or the seeming impossibilities of deliverance absorb you, nor brood over past failure, with its sin and breakdown. For every look at yourself take ten at Christ, and take strength from His Word in verse 25: ". . . thus saith the Lord, Even the captives of the mighty shall be taken away, and the prey of the terrible shall be delivered: for I will contend with him that contendeth with thee, and I will save thy children." Jesus is stronger than Satan and sin, and Satan to Jesus must bow.

The final truth, however, is perhaps the most precious of all. It is found in chapter 50:1, and it completes the picture, for it tells me that God's love is *inexhaustible in its patience*. "Thus saith the Lord, Where is the bill of your mother's divorcement, whom I have put away? or which of my creditors is it to whom I have sold you?"

Do you understand the analogy? When the Jew put away his wife, he gave her a bill of divorcement, for without that the divorce would not be complete. The people of Israel in exile are likening themselves to a divorced wife, forgotten and forsaken of God. The Lord interrupts this kind of thinking, and breaks into it with a challenge to His people, saying: "Where is the bill of divorcement? Produce it. Produce the bill and show me where I divorced you." But Israel can not do it. Of course she cannot find it, because He had never given it to her. God cannot divorce those whom He has taken into covenant relationship with Himself. They may be backslidden and rebellious, and prove faithless for a while, perhaps, but still they belong to Him. You can search everywhere, you can ransack the universe, but if you are a child of God, you will never find a bill of divorcement from God, and even the devil cannot produce it. Satan would love to do that, and to come to some disconsolate Christian who is absolutely beaten and hopeless and produce proof that God had cut him off, but he cannot do it.

This might lead someone to say, "That means there is licence for sin somewhere in the gospel." Oh, no, there isn't! If I am truly the Lord's, then His love will be in my heart and I will respond to it. I will recognize that this amazing love of God that will never let me go is that upon which I can rest everything, and count upon Him to take me out into victory. But if I am not His, then the story of that love may only harden my heart and one day prove to be the basis of my judgment. "For light is come into the world, but men prefer darkness rather than light because their deeds are evil" (*see* John 3:19). So the call comes again today. "Get out of that spiritual Babylon—quit!" What is the motive? Listen to the words of Hebrews 13 where I read in verses 12 and 13: "Jesus also, that he might sanctify the people with his own blood, suffered without the gate. Let us go forth therefore unto him without the camp, bearing his reproach." He's calling to His church, He's calling to you and to me, to a great exodus, to a great deliverance, to an escape while there is yet time, from a life of self and from the life of the world. But you only meet God outside the camp. There was a deliverance which Pharaoh offered these people once which suggested they might worship the Lord in the land, but you remember the answer of Moses, which was "No, there shall not be a hoof left behind" (*see* Exodus 10:26).

You cannot worship God while in a spiritual concentration camp! There is no place where you can meet Him save at the cross, which is outside the city wall. It is the place where you willingly and gladly say, like the prodigal, "I will arise and go to my father, and will say unto him, Father, I have sinned . . . and am no more worthy to be called thy son" (Luke 15:18, 19). But you do not only say that; you arise and go. When you do, you discover the reality of the love of God—a love that is absolutely invincible, a love that nothing ever can pass, that is absolutely infinite in its power and completely inexhaustible. But you must show that you want this with all your heart; that you are willing for the cost of complete abandonment to the lordship of Jesus Christ over every part of your life, for then, and only then, will you find a way of deliverance.

2

Isaiah 50:1-11

The Cross in the Heart of God

The Lord God hath opened mine ear, and I was not rebellious, neither turned away back. I gave my back to the smiters, and my cheeks to them that plucked off the hair: I hid not my face from shame and spitting.

Isaiah 50:5,6

This chapter is the answer of God to a people who suggested that He had cut them off and ceased to care for them. True, they were in bondage, without an altar, without a place of sacrifice, without apparent access to their God; but it was sin which had put them there. The first verse of this chapter says, "Behold, for your iniquities have ye sold yourselves, and for your transgressions is your mother put away." How often He had warned them, pleaded with them, yet there was none to answer: "Wherefore, when I came, was there no man? when I called, was there none to answer?" (v. 2). His arm was not shortened, His power was no less. Only one thing had hidden His face from them, and it is the same thing which hides the face of God from any of us—that was their sin.

How graphic is the language of verse 3: "I clothe the heavens with blackness, and I make sackcloth their covering." Oh, the sorrow in the heart of God—the pang, the pain, the agony, the suffering—when His children sin! That is what happens to our heavenly Father. We may think lightly of it, that it doesn't matter. We may excuse it and even justify it. But sin in the lives of God's people clothes heaven with blackness and sackcloth. Sin is the only thing that can do that.

20

God went even further, however, than declaring His power to save His people from this. He revealed His willingness and the lengths to which He was prepared to go, that people burdened with sin might understand that, in spite of it, God cares and loves, and He has not forsaken. Though God hates our sin, He loves the sinner, and He is never prepared to leave us to our fate, just though it might be to do so, without first of all giving us a clear revelation of His longing for our salvation.

If you have made excuses to God for your behavior, and because of it have felt forsaken of God, I want you to catch the picture that heaven is in mourning over you today. The angels weep. You may laugh it off; you can imagine that this is something which can be excused or, as I said, justified, but the rejoicing that was there over a sinner who once repented and turned to God is now silent. God has made sackcloth the covering of heaven in the breaking of His heart because of the behavior of His children. Yet, in face of this and knowing full well the facts, we complain and suggest that God does not care. So here is His answer to a complaining people.

Of course, in the mind and vision of the prophet, we are moving toward the revelation of the One who was wounded for our transgressions, who was bruised for our iniquities. That is the supreme answer of God to all our complaints and suffering. We have not reached that place yet in our studies, but we are approaching it, and chapter 50 breathes the whole atmosphere of the fact that, because we have sinned, there is a cross in the heart of God. That which we have done, which we have covered up and excused, has driven another nail into the hands of the Lord Jesus, another spear into His side.

Now, of course, we bear in mind that in his prophecy, Isaiah is referring here to the Servant of Jehovah, not Israel collectively but the Saviour personally, the One who (as chapter 49:6 reminds us) is to bring Jacob again to Himself, and is to be a Light to the Gentiles, and salvation to the ends of the earth. There are some things here in this chapter concerning our Lord that we need to reflect upon very solemnly in His presence, and in the light of them to consider our behavior.

Do we say that God does not care? Do we say that it does not matter to Him how His children act? Let me ask you to notice here what I have called the Father's commission: "The Lord

God hath given me the tongue of the learned, that I should know how to speak a word in season to him that is weary: he wakeneth morning by morning, he wakeneth mine ear to hear as the learned" (v. 4).

At the back of all our complaints that God forgets and does not care is something that is described for us in this verse—weariness.

I suppose we all know something at one stage or another of physical weariness, mental fatigue, and what it is to be heartsick. But I think the greatest weariness of all comes upon a man who becomes weary in the battle of life, the battle he has with himself and his sin. Oh, how often he has longed that somehow he might make one mighty attack upon the devil and be done with him forever! Instead of that the conflict has been incessant. To defeat him today only invites a renewed attack tomorrow in some more subtle guise. So it goes on day after day and the ordeal is continuous, while beneath the ordeal, heart and flesh have often failed. "Oh, God, is there no release from this?" There is nothing new in that.

Weariness in the conflict against sin is not exclusive, and we are reminded in Romans 8:22 that the whole creation groans and travails together in pain until now. Oh, the awful weariness of sin! There has never been a time, perhaps, when it is so obvious and evident as it is in this day in which we live, with the sheer fatigue and heartsickness with it all.

Into such a world the Father sent His Son, and He sent Him to speak a word in season to them that are weary in the battle. The thought, of course, in this fourth verse, is that before the Son could speak that word to us, He must first be identified Himself with our weariness.

So we see His preparation for this great task. Though He were a Son, says the writer to the Hebrews, He learned obedience by the things that He suffered, and He passed through every stage and every sphere of human experience and exhaustion. Let me remind you and allow the Holy Spirit to speak to you about this, the Lord (whom we say has forgotten), being wearied with His journey, sat by a well. On another occasion He looked up to heaven and sighed because of the unbelief of the people: "O faithless and perverse generation, how long shall I be with you? how long shall I suffer you?" (Matthew 17:17).

Heartsickness and weariness in the battle with the thing that has defeated us, fatigue in this spiritual conflict, made Him stumble one day under the sheer load and fall as He carried His cross up toward the green hill outside Jerusalem. It was relentless all through His life. He was constantly learning that, morning by morning, His Father awakened His ear to hear, as those that are being taught obedience.

Think again of a brief snatch of sleep the Lord had somewhere on a mountainside or by the lakeshore, occasionally in the home in Bethany, when He would be wakened by a voice speaking from the glory, morning by morning, bringing to Him constantly the shadow of the cross from which there was no escape. "Never man spake like this man" (John 7:46), exclaimed the people, but it was because every morning the Father awakened Him to speak to Him afresh, and what the Son heard in the ear He proclaimed from the housetops, as He prepared for the great task of our salvation. Such was the Father's commission.

Consider now the Son's obedience in verse 5: "The Lord God hath opened mine ear, and I was not rebellious, neither turned away back." Every day the Father poured into His heart the necessity of Calvary, that He must suffer and die. The Lord Jesus could never be God's answer to the weariness and sinfulness of the whole human race merely by His enduring hardness. He must go all the way: He must bleed, He must be made sin, He must be identified with the horror and evil of it, He must take it all at the cross. From His birth to His death, Calvary was constantly borne upon His heart, and He anticipated all the suffering.

Think of the shame He endured, the spitting, the scourging, the dying on the cross. He was not rebellious, neither did He turn away back, but always set His face steadfastly toward Jerusalem and the ultimate goal of God's purpose for His life.

My friends, when you and I sin, we sin against that. May God forgive us! We say He doesn't care; we say He has forgotten us. While heaven mourns and the angels weep, we go on living in our self-centered way. He turned not away, nor was He rebellious, because He loved. How amazing that He loved to such a degree people like us!

We have thought of the Father's commission, the Son's obedience, and now meditate on the Servant's suffering: "I gave my back to the smiters, and my cheeks to them that plucked off the hair: I hid not my face from shame and spitting" (v. 6).

Obedience involved for Jesus suffering like that—insult, shame, cruelty, and finally death—but He endured it, and He endured it voluntarily: "I *gave* my back to the smiters." He looked down the corridors of time for two thousand years, and He had you and me in His heart. He saw the life we lived, the sin we committed, our failure and breakdown. He heard all our excusing of it and our self-justification. He listened as we vindicated ourselves, saying, "It doesn't matter how I live, for God has forgotten; He doesn't care. I can get away with things for nobody knows and nobody minds."

Ah, but the Lord *did* care: He gave His back to the smiters. One flash of His majesty and authority and those who captured Him would have fallen on their faces before Him. They could not have touched Him had He not consented. But instead He allowed them to blindfold Him; they buffeted and struck Him; they spat in His face. In the midst of humiliation He said to Pilate, "Thou couldest have no power at all against me, except it were given thee from above" (John 19:11).

So we behold our precious Lord Jesus exposing His majestic face to shame and spitting. That dear, sweet face has been wet with tears for you and me and a sinful world, a face the like of which humanity has never gazed upon before in its beauty and loveliness, strength and power and meekness. Yes, and that is the same face from which, when He comes in glory and majesty and power, heaven and earth will flee away, and people will cry out for the rocks to hide them. The face of Jesus, once marred in humiliation, will be the majestic focus of all eternity.

As I think of His suffering, somehow I know that it was not the nails that riveted Him to the cross, but it was His passion for the glory of God at any cost, and His undying love for men who were rebelling against Him because He was holy, and challenging them to that kind of life, too.

Was it the nails, O Saviour, that bound Thee to the tree?
Nay, 'twas Thy everlasting love, Thy love for me, for me.

K. A. M. KELLY

Friend, are you still saying that God has forgotten, and therefore you can justify your conduct?

Let me say to you with much conviction in my heart as I do, that if you don't look up into that lovely face quickly and say, "Lord Jesus, I acknowledge that I am a sinner. I have been hiding it and covering it in the name of religion and Christian profession. Under a cloak of sympathy for other people I have allowed myself to be carried away into the worst form of failure and sin"—then the day of grace may be over for you.

If you do not look up into His face and tell Him the whole story *now* and see Him look down on you with love and grace and forgiving mercy, then one day those eyes like a flame of fire will look into the depth of your soul and you will flee away in vain from them. It will be too late then. Let me tell you that God is going to have the last word about your sin, not you. May He have mercy upon us.

The final picture is of the Saviour's victory: "For the Lord God will help me; therefore shall I not be confounded: therefore have I set my face like a flint, and I know that I shall not be ashamed" (v. 7).

Notice that the tone is changing in this chapter. The Saviour's previous words were full of submission and tender, patient suffering. We have been taken in this chapter into Gethsemane; we have watched Him going up the green hill; we have seen it all. This is holy ground, for the eternal God has permitted us to peer, as it were, into the very heart of His suffering Son, allowed us to listen to what is going on in His very soul as He went alone up a lonely road to a cross. "I have set my face like a flint, and I know that I shall not be ashamed. He is near that justifieth me; who will contend with me? let us stand together: who is mine adversary? let him come near to me. Behold, the Lord God will help me; who is he that shall condemn me? lo, they all shall wax old as a garment; the moth shall eat them up" (*see* vs. 7-9).

Do you still say that God doesn't care?

"My God, my God, why hast thou forsaken me?" (Matthew 27:46) was the central cry upon the cross, and here is the echo of it. In it all there is a ring of determination. Listen to Him as He treads the winepress alone; as He trudges that weary journey up to the cross alone; as He bears the agony of a fearful death and faces that awful last stage of the conflict; as He takes the cup the Father has given Him, to drink it to the very dregs that there might not be left one drop for us to drink, that we might be free from all judgment. "Thy will, not mine, be done," He said (*see* Matthew 26:42).

He could have called twelve legions of angels to deliver Him, but He faced the whole ordeal alone. Just picture the Lord Jesus in Pilate's hall with Peter outside denying Him, the disciples running away, Judas betraying Him with a kiss, with all his profession of love and belief—and there Jesus Christ stands in the place of shame and humiliation. All the while His heart is proclaiming, ". . . the Lord God will help me; therefore shall I not be confounded: therefore have I set my face like a flint, and I know that I shall not be ashamed" (v. 7).

In the uttermost depths of the moment which meant our redemption, when He had gone right down there to prove to us all that He cares, He is sure and confident of victory. This is so because His confidence is based upon His Father's help, and faith in His help is based on confidence in His Father's will.

At that moment as our Saviour was being brought lower and lower, facing sin and being made sin for us, His whole life constituted a claim upon God that He could not deny. There is absolute confidence of ultimate triumph here. The possibility of failure at the last minute never occurred to Him, for the Son of man *must* suffer many things, *must* be killed, and *must* be raised again—". . . who for the joy that was set before him endured the cross, despising the shame, and is set down at the right hand of the throne of God" (Hebrews 12:2).

Yes, the cross was always before Him, but so was the empty tomb. He was always sure of His ability to fulfill the purpose of His coming as a ransom for many. He was sure that God would vindicate Him. "He is near that justifieth me," He said. "He is near that vindicates" is more accurate, not 'justifies' in the sense of making Him righteous, but vindicating His name. Through all the suffering, the infamous trial, all the way along the road to Calvary, He stayed Himself by saying, "He is near; who is he that condemns? It is God that justifies."

The world mocked Him in saying, "He is a friend of sinners!" God justified Him by saying, "If He is the friend of sinners, He is that in order to make sinners saints."

The world has said He was mad, but God justified Him, and has done so ever since, in making the teaching of Jesus Christ to be the light of every soul that has trusted Him.

The world said, "He has a devil!" But God vindicated Him by giving Him the power to cast out every demon and evil thing!

The world said He blasphemed when He called Himself the Son of God. God justified Him by raising Him from the dead in order that one day He will return in the clouds from heaven with great glory as King of kings.

What has this to say to your heart today? My heart is deeply stirred as I think about the cross. Is yours? That is what it cost Jesus, and that is what He thought about sin. That is what it meant to Him to face all He went through and endured for our redemption. If you can still say He has forgotten, He doesn't care, He will excuse you, if you can go on sinning in the light of that, God have mercy on you.

What is the appeal to your life in this? It is twofold, and in the first place it is an appeal to identification with our Lord. There are limits, of course, beyond which no human being can go, but I think the Lord is saying to our hearts again today that this is the way the Master trod in preparation for His commission in the words of Isaiah 50:4. If you have come to the cross for redemption, you must come to it also for identification: "I am crucified with Christ: nevertheless I live; yet not I, but Christ liveth in me: and the life which I now live in the flesh I live by the faith of the Son of God, who loved me, and gave himself for me" (Galatians 2:20). This means that we must tread the Calvary road, too. He wants to give us the tongue of those that are taught. He wants to give us the ability to speak a word in season to the man who is weary in the battle of life. To do this He will awaken us morning by morning to speak the word of the cross into our ears, and He expects us to share and identify with Him. As we take the scoffing, the reviling and persecution of other people, making ourselves but a doormat for Jesus, here surely is an appeal to identification.

There is also an appeal, to those who say that God has forgotten, to put their trust in Him. See the language of verse 10: "Who is among you that feareth the Lord, that obeyeth the voice of his servant, that walketh in darkness, and hath no light? let him trust in the name of the Lord, and stay upon his God."

Are you in the dark just now? If so, that may be because of the attitudes of which I have been speaking: "Behold, all ye that kindle a fire, that compass yourselves about with sparks: walk in the light of your fire, and in the sparks that ye have kindled. This shall ye have of mine hand; ye shall lie down in sorrow" (v. 11). Yes, you can try to get out of the dark by evading the real issue and make your own sparks to guide your life. But there is another way: he that walks in darkness and has no light, let him trust in the Lord (*see* v. 10). For the Lord God will help you, therefore you will not be confounded and therefore you, like Jesus, may set your face like a flint, and you, too, will know that you shall never be ashamed.

If you are prepared honestly to accept, as Jesus Christ did, this principle of a life of utter submission and preparation in order that He might fulfill the Father's commission and be made sin for us, then just as His life made a claim upon the power and intervention and ability of heaven, so will yours.

If you are prepared to walk the Calvary road today, recognizing that you have been excusing and justifying yourself, if you now repent and turn to God in complete trust and submission, and resolve to walk with Him, then I tell you, that constitutes a demand upon the throne in heaven. It is the man who is repentant and broken who is guaranteed the outpouring of the Holy Spirit in his life constantly, no one else. It is a life of submission to the will of God that can lay claim upon all the power of the risen Lord, which He died and rose again to make available and possible, in order that through such a life there may come the authority of the risen and indwelling Christ.

> I cannot tell how silently He suffered,
>   As with His peace He graced this place of tears,
> Or how His heart upon the Cross was broken,
>   The crown of pain to three and thirty years.

But this I know, He heals the broken-hearted,
And stays our sin, and calms our lurking fear,
And lifts the burden from the heavy laden,
For yet the Saviour, Saviour of the world, is here.

                                        W.Y. FULLERTON

3

Isaiah 51

The Call of God—Retrospect and Prospect

Hearken to me, ye that follow after righteousness, ye that seek the Lord: look unto the rock whence ye are hewn, and to the hole of the pit whence ye are digged.

Isaiah 51:1

It is necessary to be reminded of the context of Isaiah 51. God has issued the people of Israel a clarion call to take action about their present position. The time of their captivity was coming to an end and in chapter 48:20 we read: "Go ye forth of Babylon, flee ye from the Chaldeans, with a voice of singing declare ye, tell this, utter it even to the end of the earth; say ye, The Lord hath redeemed his servant Jacob." This was the divine order to move out from their captivity and return to the land of blessing and promise.

This command of God, however, was met by a complaint as expressed in chapter 49:14, "But Zion said, The Lord hath forsaken me, and my Lord hath forgotten me."

"What's the use?" the people say, "Seventy years of bondage in Babylon, seventy years under the chastisement of a holy God, seventy years out of blessing and cast aside, without the breath of God upon our lives—what's the use? He has forgotten and forsaken us; He doesn't care."

Immediately the response of the Lord comes in Isaiah 49:16, "Behold, I have graven thee upon the palms of my hands; thy walls are continually before me." He does not say "thy ruins" but "thy walls"—not what you have been, but what I intended

30

you to be, and I have never lost sight of that. He iterates His love for His people, as we saw in the previous study in Isaiah 50:4, "The Lord God hath given me the tongue of the learned, that I should know how to speak a word in season to him that is weary: he wakeneth morning by morning, he wakeneth mine ear to hear as the learned."

Once a Christian becomes eaten up with discouragement and unbelief it takes a great deal to shake him out of it. Those two emotions are the masterstrokes of Satan. So long as the child of God maintains an attitude of praise and trust in the Lord, then he is invincible. Once the devil gets him discouraged, that poor man is really going to take a knocking!

Now, in Isaiah 51, there is a word for the person who is discouraged and downhearted, who thinks, "What's the use, anyway?" For notwithstanding the promises of deliverance from exile and the summons to depart, the Israelites could not bring themselves to believe that they would ever be of any use to the Lord again. They remembered the broken walls and desolation of their beloved Jerusalem and felt the situation to be hopeless.

I am so glad that I know a Saviour who restores the wasted and unfruitful years. When I know Him in a deep personal way, I know with all my heart it is never too late to begin again. Bless the Lord!

A further call of God comes to us afresh in what I have called "Retrospect and Prospect"; a subheading might be "A Word to the Downhearted." God brings His people to recognize their position, and He speaks to them in this chapter by asking them to look back at the past, to look on to the future, and in the recognition of the past and in the assurance of the future, to stand their ground today.

Three times in Isaiah 51:1-8 the voice of God calls to His people, "Hearken to me" (vs. 1,4,7). It is as if He is saying, "You have listened to practically every other voice you can—to Job's comforters, to the inward whisper of the devil saying the situation is useless, to folk who would discourage—now hearken to Me."

There is always a precious orderliness in everything God says. He never speaks out of order, He never puts first things last or last things first. In the first verse of this chapter He says, "Hearken to me," and who is to listen? "You who follow after righteousness and seek the Lord." In verse 4 He says, "Hearken unto me, my people"; and in verse 7 He says, "Hearken unto me, ye that know righteousness, the people in whose heart is my law."

What a wonderful sequence! If I follow after righteousness, this is an indication that God has put a hunger for Himself in my heart, and I am His. Because I am His, therefore I will know His righteousness, and His law will be in my heart. God is always orderly.

What then does He say to those who follow after righteousness, and by so doing indicate that they are His and are seeking to obey Him from the heart? In the first place He says, "Stop and look back . . . look unto the rock whence ye are hewn, and to the hole of the pit whence ye are digged" (*see* v. 1).

To a nation reduced at this time to a mere handful, under the tyranny of a power that seems to be utterly overwhelming, and from whom rescue seems impossible, the Lord says, "Before you take such a defeatist attitude, go back to the beginning of My dealings with you, and look at the rock from which I hewed you, and the pit from which I dug you. Remember the lowliness and obscurity of your origin."

It is good for us to do that, as it deepens our humility and magnifies the grace of God. I pray unceasingly that God will show to me all the possibilities in my heart because, believe me, they are all in the downward direction. There are very strong ties to the pit from which we were dug, and very often we are ashamed of our likeness to the family from which God has saved us. It is good to look back, for in so doing none of us can boast of any transformation in our lives because, if there is any difference, God has done it all. If you look back to the origin of our salvation, to the beginning of our redemption, if He has done so much, then bless the Lord, He will complete what He has done. He never leaves a task half-finished. If the stone has been hewn out of the rock, it can be polished. If He has justified us, then He can sanctify us. If, when we were enemies, we were reconciled to God by the death of His Son, much more, being reconciled, we shall be saved by His life (*see* Romans 5:10).

So it is for their encouragement that Israel is urged to take a backward look, and even though they are only a handful in number now, they are more than that with which God began, for He started their history with one man.

"But, Lord," they say to Him, "the pruning and the cutting down are so merciless, the disciplines have been so hard to take, and the punishment has been almost more than we can bear, that quite frankly the flesh groans under it all."

God replies, "See how I dealt with Abraham: Look unto Abraham your father, and unto Sarah that bare you" (*see* v. 2).

God called Abraham *alone*, says the Scripture. And in the process of that call his father Terah died. His nephew Lot dropped out by the wayside as the pace became too hot for him. His wife's plan that Abram should have a child by another woman, in order to hasten the promise of God, fell apart. Isaac the child of promise was laid on the altar, and Abraham's faith was tried almost beyond endurance. Twenty-five years had passed between the time of the Lord's promise of a child and the actual birth. By that time natural force was spent, and then when the child was born there came (may I say it reverently?) the ridiculous command, from the human angle, to slay the child of promise. It was as if God gave Abraham that which He promised, and then was about to take it away in order to teach the man that the Lord must be all in all. For he was to be the father of a great nation, in whom all families of the world would be blessed, and therefore he must be one from whom every bit of confidence in the flesh had been stripped so that he might die to himself. The writer of the Hebrew Epistle said this of him, "By faith Abraham, when he was tried, offered up Isaac: and he that had received the promises offered up his only begotten son, Of whom it was said, That in Isaac shall thy seed be called: accounting that God was able to raise him up, even from the dead; from whence also he received him in a figure" (Hebrews 11:17-19).

"Now," says the Lord to His discouraged people, "after all these years of testing and trial, look back to the way in which I began with you."

God is asking some depressed, disheartened Christian to do this very thing, for the way in which God dealt with Abraham is exactly the way in which He deals with you and me.

As He takes His child to be His own, and when that man is born of the Spirit, He begins at that very moment to cut down to the root his very self-life until He strips him of pride and prestige. There must be nothing of self in his life to hinder his progress. There has to be the destruction of every bit of self-confidence in order that he might wait solely upon the Lord for the abounding inflow of His grace and power. God has no taste for battalions or regiments. He chooses an Abraham, a Gideon or a Luther, Livingstone, Carey, Wesley, Judson, Brainard, Moody. And through one man who has followed and accepted the principles of His dealings and who has stood, as it were, under the pruning knife, through that man God has brought whole nations to the feet of Jesus Christ, to be renewed and redeemed by His precious blood.

Are you feeling the hopelessness of your case today? Are you feeling under a cloud, and that it is useless to try to continue your profession of faith? Then look back and remember the pit. Consider the grace of God. Do you feel just a tiny channel for His blessing, and therefore imagine you do not count? The whole ocean of His fullness can be poured into your life. The question is not what you can do or what you cannot do, at this point, but what are you willing for God to do? The only condition of accomplishment is His presence in your heart and life.

Something happens to the Christian who recognizes this, as is seen in Isaiah 51:3: "For the Lord shall comfort Zion: he will comfort all her waste places; and he will make her wilderness like Eden, and her desert like the garden of the Lord; joy and gladness shall be found therein, thanksgiving, and the voice of melody."

Consider some of the words used: *waste places, wilderness, desert:* does that describe you? Is that your life, a waste place, a wilderness, a desert before God? But here is His promise to the man who is utterly discouraged: "The Lord . . . will comfort. . . . he will make [the] wilderness like Eden and [the] desert like the garden of the Lord." He asks you, therefore, today, if you are discouraged as a Christian and on the point of giving up, to look back to the pit from which He digged you, and to reckon upon His unfailing love.

But He asks you to do something else, to look on to future glory. "Hearken unto me, my people; and give ear unto me, O my nation. . . . My righteousness is near; my salvation is gone forth, and mine arms shall judge the people; the isles shall wait upon me, and on mine arm shall they trust. Lift up your eyes to the heavens, and look upon the earth beneath: for the heavens shall vanish away like smoke, and the earth shall wax old like a garment, and they that dwell therein shall die in like manner: but my salvation shall be for ever, and my righteousness shall not be abolished" (vs. 4-6).

"My salvation shall be for ever—my righteousness shall not be abolished"—what is God saying? In the midst of your testing and discouragement, the things that make you feel so hopeless as you have taken a good look back at the pit, now He bids you look up to the heavens and look down to the earth. Well, they seem solid enough, no change can come to them! Oh, yes, it can, and indeed it will. For the Bible tells us that one day there will be a new heaven and a new earth, as the order we now know becomes old as a garment. Amidst the wreck and judgment which will surely come one day, God's salvation remains. We don't know how long the world will continue as it is, nor how long it will be before the unveiling of the Lord. We don't know how long before the King shall come, or when His great judgment day will dawn. We don't know how long before the resurrection of the living and the dead, or when all the elements shall burn up, as Peter himself tells us. But this we do know, that the Lord Jesus Christ and His redeemed people endure through it all. They are accepted in Him; they are washed in His blood. They are members of His body and of one another. They are the bride of Christ, and are absolutely indestructible no matter what may happen all around. The Lord Himself sees them through. So He says to His people who are discouraged, "Look on!"

You see, when you and I partake of Jesus and He becomes part of our lives, we acquire someone in our hearts who is permanent, and who defies time and change and circumstance, whatever they may be. He has come to stay. It is not what you possess that lasts, but what you *are.* Jesus Christ has come by His Spirit to live in your heart in order to produce within you that life which can never be destroyed. And just what is that life? It is the love of God shed abroad in our hearts by His Spirit, and it is also our love one for the other. It is the patience and strength, the courage and faith which are acquired in the midst of a furnace of trial. These things do not vanish in a puff of smoke. If they did, what would be the use of God's painstaking care over His people?

It is as if we are now in school, and we shall continue there until we get to heaven. The school may vanish or crash around us, but that which we have learned and acquired into heart and life while there will remain forever.

Christian, don't complain at God's slow progress in educating His children. Do not murmur at the care He takes over His people to be sure they master each lesson. Have you noticed how the Lord takes us back again and again over the same ground until we almost cry aloud as we say, "But Lord, I have learned that lesson!" He knows we have not reached the place of perfect knowledge, so He brings us back again to the beginning until His instruction becomes part of our very life. The Lord is not a university professor teaching us for a life-span of seventy years or so; He is God Eternal training us for eternity.

Therefore, do not complain at the care He takes. He is working with an eternal purpose in view, for a man's life does not consist of that which he possesses, but it consists of meekness, faith, devotion, love, consecration, dedication, Christlikeness. Believe me, many a man has forfeited everything of the material, that he might find in his life the reality of the Saviour. Is that your attitude and desire?

"I count all things but loss," says the Apostle Paul, "for the excellency of the knowledge of Christ Jesus my Lord: for whom I have suffered the loss of all things, and do count them but dung, that I may win Christ, And be found in him, not having mine own righteousness, which is of the law, but that which is through the faith of Christ, the righteousness which is of God by faith: That I may know him, and the power of his resurrection, and the fellowship of his sufferings, being made conformable unto his death" (Philippians 3:8-10).

Yes, we are at school today, and in the midst of discouragement and disappointment, we hear the Lord say, "Look back— but look on."

All you may see is the immediate test and trial, that from which you would give almost anything to escape, but God says, "Look on! Be patient! I am not training you for a little while down here, but to prepare you to be with Me forever in glory; and that takes time and diligence. I have to take you back time and again to the kindergarten, over the same ground many times until, when you ultimately see Me face-to-face, I shall know that you have learned the lesson."

"Hearken unto me," says the Lord. "Look at the pit. Hearken unto me, look at the glory. Hearken unto me, stand your ground: Hearken unto me, ye that know righteousness, the people in whose heart is my law; fear ye not the reproach of men, neither be ye afraid of their revilings" (v. 7).

Now at first sight it may seem very unusual to link the two thoughts in the one verse: men in whose heart is the law of God and (in the next breath) men who are filled with revilings on their account. But stop a moment and check this with your own experience.

First we read of the man in whose heart is the law of God, that is, the man who is born again of the Spirit, and because of that glorious fact he is living a different life. He has a new power imparted to him, and a new principle by which to live victoriously. He has remembered the pit; he looks forward to the glory; now he is going through the school, bearing the testings and trials. They have a new significance now, for he sees the Lord has him in His hand refining the gold, sanctifying him once he is justified in order to present him one day faultless in His presence. So now the believer is being schooled by the Spirit because of what he has already experienced of the grace of God, and he is therefore living his life on a completely new principle through the power of the Holy Spirit let loose within him.

Inevitably such a man clashes with the ungodly. Perhaps I should put it this way: inevitably the ungodly man clashes with him. When I say, "ungodly," I do not mean someone immoral, but what the word says, *ungodly*, without God. Anyone who lives in the power of God's Spirit, who has the law of God, not in his head but in his heart, who is living out this principle of the Christian life in the power of His indwelling, with eternity in view—immediately that person collides with every ungodly man he meets. The ungodly, you see, react in self-defense. Either they are right and the believer is wrong, or the Christian is right and they are wrong; and as they are not prepared to admit that they are wrong, in self-defense and in order to establish and justify their position, and to destroy every evidence of spiritual value, they will come into a confrontation with the man who is godly.

Let me say something very quietly but very firmly: if that is not happening in your life as a believer, examine yourself that you are in the faith, that you are a child of God. The godly man in whose life is the law of God and who is living in the power of the Spirit is such a rebuke to the ungodly that the moment the ungodly see him and recognize the principles upon which he is living and the new standards of his life, they begin to revile in order to justify their position.

"Hearken unto me, ye that know righteousness. . . . fear ye not the reproach of men, neither be ye afraid of their revilings." If I am related by grace to the living God I am not afraid of a dying man. In Matthew 5:11, 12 we read, "Blessed [happy] are ye, when men shall revile you, and persecute you, and shall say all manner of evil against you falsely, for my sake. Rejoice, and be exceeding glad: for great is your reward in heaven."

A word of caution is in place here. If you suffer because you are a mean sort of Christian, do not try and shelter under that text, will you? If you suffer because you are inconsistent or thoughtless, because you are always pushing a tract at people and asking, "Brother, are you saved?" then do not expect to get anything less than you deserve. Do not misunderstand me: I think it is a very good thing to hand out tracts, but I think in doing so you must be very sure that you are revealing the grace and loveliness and sweetness of Jesus Christ in your approach. If there is something about your Christianity that is unattractive and repulsive, then don't complain if people are constantly reviling you. Ah, but if you are living with the law of God in your heart, and love has gripped your life, and you are obeying Him, then you are blessed when men say all manner of evil against you falsely, for great is your reward in heaven.

Stand your ground, therefore, and allow the life of the risen Lord Jesus to flow through you so that reviling tongues may be silenced, and His power acknowledged as being the force of your life.

4

Isaiah 51:9-52:11

It Is Time to Wake Up

Awake, awake, put on strength, O arm of the Lord.

Isaiah 51:9

Awake, awake, put on thy strength, O Zion.

Isaiah 52:1

Three times in the early part of Isaiah 51 God calls His people to hearken. But He seems to be speaking to a people incapable of response (vs. 17-19). They are addressed as if stupified by strong drink, having drunk at the hand of the Lord the cup of His fury. There is none to take them by the hand and guide them back to God, no one to show them the way of blessing. From such a people comes at last a cry for God's intervention in verse 9, which seems justified for it is based on past experience (v. 10). The Lord delivered from Egypt, so surely He can do so from Babylon. He dried up the waters of the Red Sea; surely He can now make His mountains a way. Past experience of God's blessing is always a strong argument for faith for today. All that seemed to be needed was a flash of His mighty power, apparently lying dormant, and all His enemies, and theirs, would be scattered. "O Lord, awake and save us!" is their cry.

The Bible is amazingly up-to-date. It seems to be a living commentary on current events, and because it is just that, it has the only answer to our basic problems. So first notice here *the period of spiritual depression.*

God's ideal for His children in relation to growth is steady, consistent progress in attaining their objective, which is conformity to Himself. But does it ever happen like that? History and experience answer *no*. Winter and summer have been in all our lives. There have been days when a cold chill seems to grip our hearts, and heaven is hidden: times when our faith loses its grip, our love its glow, our service its enthusiasm, when we become bound to convention and our souls seem to have frozen up. What has been true individually is also true in the ebb and flow of church history. There have been periods when the tide has receded so far that there appeared to be no turning, but in His mercy God has moved in once more in revival blessing.

Here we are today, with our machinery, our money, our organization and our western culture, yet as individuals and as churches we are spiritually at a desperately low ebb. "Ye have sown much, and bring in little" (Haggai 1:6).

Now such a period of spiritual depression can only have one or the other of two outcomes. Either it becomes deeper until sleep ends in death, or it is broken up by a new outburst of spiritual life and vitality. Would to God that our spiritual growth had been steady! But if it has not—and let us confess this to be more often the case—then the resumption of growth is the only alternative to rotting away.

Truths which for years have lost their hold upon us can flame up into a fire which burns within to cause us to march in obedience and love to God. The air becomes electric, the fire begins to spread, and a mighty spiritual advance is made in a day. "It is time for thee, Lord, to work" (Psalm 119:126).

Charles Finney defines revival as the renewal of the first love of Christians, resulting in the conversion of sinners to God. It presupposes that the church is backslidden, and revival means conviction of sin and searching of heart among God's people. Revival is nothing less than a new beginning of obedience to God—a breaking of heart and getting down into the dust before Him, with deep humility and forsaking of sin. A revival breaks the power of the world and of sin over Christians. The charm of the world is broken, and the power of sin is overcome. Truths to which our hearts are unresponsive suddenly become living. Whereas mind and conscience may assent to truth, when revival comes, obedience to the truth is the one thing that matters.

Does your heart beat in eager response to those words? There can be evangelism without that, but until God moves in melting, moving power in His church, His people are helpless to face the challenge of the times, and are bankrupt of resources to live as Christians are intended to live in the light of the cross.

Here, in our study of the prophecy of Isaiah, is a captive people crying to God that His power, which is unchanging and unending, might flame into action and shatter the walls of their prison. Though His power is unchanging, the expression and display of it constantly changes. The force remains the same, but the amount brought into action varies according to our readiness to receive it. If God appears to slumber it is primarily because we do (see v. 17 and chapter 52:1). His arm is not shortened that it cannot save; He that keeps Israel shall neither slumber nor sleep. But He works through us, and if the law of the spirit of life in Christ seems almost to have died out in you, the fault is not in Him.

We have the solemn and awful power of checking the life of God which would flow through us, of limiting the Holy One of Israel. Our capacity determines the amount we receive, and our desire determines our capacity. God gives as much of Himself as we will, as much as we can hold, and there is always so much more that we could have had if only we would. "Ye are not straitened in me, ye are straitened in yourselves" (see 2 Corinthians 6:12).

Let us be honest: if we lament times of spiritual depression, let us acknowledge where the fault lies. If God's arm seems inactive, it is because we are asleep. Repeated struggles to free ourselves from captivity have been in vain. His power never changes; the gospel committed to His people has lost none of its infallible power, but we see little of its fruit, and need we wonder?

Of course, there is always plenty of activity, many spiritual ventures and generous giving. But how little communion with God! How little unworldly elevation of soul! How little glow of love! An improvement of social position, a type of higher education from the pulpit, beautiful buildings, refinement of music and forms of worship—what tragically poor substitutes these are for what we have lost in chasing after them! Surely we do not really believe the answer to our need is in any of them.

We have the mantle of Elijah, the outward resemblance to the fathers who have gone, but the fire has returned to heaven with them. Soft and weak as we are, we stand on the brink of the river invoking the Lord God of Elijah: but the floods pay no attention. Commercial prosperity, business cares, artistic culture, and much more eat the very life out of us and chill our fervor.

I am not flinging out censure on anyone. I am merely giving voice to the confession of my own heart, and I believe of many of you, in order that we may hasten back to the Lord whom we have left to serve alone, as the disciples did in the Garden while they lay sleeping.

> O Breath of Life, come sweeping through us.
> Revive Thy Church with life and power;
> O Breath of Life, come, cleanse, renew us
> And fit Thy Church to meet this hour.
>
> BESSIE PORTER HEAD

Yet things like this are happening at the present time. Let me tell you about one church on the West Coast of the United States which suddenly found itself flung out of a state of depressing normalcy into one of thrilling renewal. A hippie wandered into the church one day, to the surprise and, if I may say so, disapproval of the two hundred fifty or so church members. He was soundly converted, and the pastor suggested that rather than conform to a traditional church program he go out to witness to his own people. Some weeks later he returned with about two dozen similar young people—jeans, T-shirts, beads, headbands, bare feet, the lot. The church members were scandalized, especially as the young people did not know how to behave in church, and sat with their feet up on the seats in front of them, poking their toes through the communion-glass holders!

The following Sunday the pastor found a notice in the foyer

of the church, No Bare Feet. After the service he called a church meeting, and said, in effect, either that notice was removed or he ceased to be pastor. He won the day, and soon the little neighborhood church was bursting at the seams, teeming with thrilling young life. What was he to do? How could he accommodate the increasing numbers? The answer was a tent, and when I visited that church some five years after the youth explosion, I attended a Saturday night meeting in which there were over three thousand people, the vast majority under twenty-five years of age. They sat spellbound for over three hours listening to some wonderfully worshipful music played and sung by young people who, up to a few years previously, had been high on drugs and sex, and then an expository study of the Word of God for about one and one-half hours by the pastor. This is typical of what goes on every night of the week, when some two thousand young people—a different group each night—meet simply to study God's Word. These thrilling sessions are led by the pastor and his assistants, and as in the early days of the Christian church, souls are being added to that church daily.

See what follows: *the prayer for spiritual recovery* (v. 9). Now of course the sure sign that revival is on the way is that in desperation we cry out to God for it. The first sign of life with a child, as with the church, is a cry! As the mother hears that cry amid all household duties, so our Father God hears the cry of His child who has lost hold of His hand, even amidst the praises surrounding His throne, which are as the sound of many waters.

Every stirring of spiritual awakening begins with the painful discovery of the wretched deadness of the past. We gaze like a man asleep, and walk towards the abyss into which one more step would hurl us, before we cry, "Lord, save me!"

His power flows into us in the measure of our longing and desire. We are told in some quarters that we are wrong to pray for an outpouring of the Holy Spirit because ever since Pentecost the church has possessed that gift. Factually that is true, but the conclusion drawn from the fact is wrong.

The Holy Spirit is not given like a bag of money put into our hand once for all, but rather as a constant communication to be received and retained according to our deep desire and constant faithfulness. You might as well say, why ask for natural life, having received it several years ago? Yes, but for every moment of those years you have continued to live, not because of a past gift, but because at each moment God breathes into you the breath of life.

So it is in the life of the Holy Spirit. We must continually and eagerly receive what He is ready to impart, otherwise we perish. There is no substitute at all for this, and without it we are lost, no matter how fine our performance or how good our technique. Professional Christianity in whatever form—preaching, music, witness, or anything else—is the greatest enemy to spiritual power. All this has dulled our appetite for the things of the Lord, and winter in our soul has been far too long a season.

Our work for God has been done with all too little sense of our need of His blessing, with little deep desire for His power. We have prayed lazily, scarcely believing an answer would come. Words have become mechanical, prayers conventional, just syllables winged with no faith or devotion. Is this a picture of your prayer life? No wonder it seems to rise into empty air and produces so little fruit, as you look squarely at the bleak fact of prayerless Bible reading and faithless praying.

Oh, that a heaven-piercing cry like that which captive Israel sent up out of weary bondage might rend the heavens from your heart: "Awake, awake, put on [thy] strength, O arm of the Lord!"

The age of miracles is not gone! The great evidences of His power in the spread of the gospel in the past is His pattern for the future. We can base our cry to God on His unchangeableness. Think of the prayers of the Lord Jesus Himself: even He, who needed no cleansing, who was always about His Father's business, how He prayed!

When He began His ministry, at the close of the first day, He was found in prayer in a desert place. When He would send forth His disciples, He spent the night alone in prayer. When the crowd wanted to make Him the center of political revolution, He sent them away and departed to a mountain to pray. When He stooped at the grave of Lazarus before raising him to life again, He prayed. Then He crowned it all with that wonderful prayer for His disciples and us in John 17. In the Garden He prayed; on the cross eclipsed by darkness He prayed. Yes, and even in *His* life the unmeasured possession of Holy Spirit power was an answer to His prayer, for "it came to pass, that Jesus also being baptized, and praying, the heaven was opened, And the Holy Ghost descended in a bodily shape like a dove upon him" (Luke 3:21,22).

Now look at the outcome, *the power of God revealed* (Isaiah 52:1). God's awakening is in fact our waking. He puts on strength by making us strong. He clothes Himself with our weakness, and answers our cry by imparting His life and strength constantly to us as we maintain our communion with Him and keep the channel clean. That simply means the active employment of our whole being with His truth and with Himself: the mind accepting the principles of His Word, the heart beating in time with the very heart of God, the will laying its hand in His, every passion knowing His finger to be in control.

That is what is implied in this verse: ". . . put on thy strength, O Zion; put on thy beautiful garments, O Jerusalem." Not only garments, but beautiful garments! Yes, the beauty of the Lord our God must be upon us. We cannot manufacture such apparel, for it is compassion, kindness, humility, meekness, long-suffering—the fruit of the Spirit outlined in Galatians 5:22,23. They are all prepared for us in Christ, and we put on our beautiful garments by putting on Christ, taking Him to be for us what God has made Him.

None of the Lord's people need go round in spiritual rags. None need be clothed in anything less than the light with which He clothed Himself: "[Thou] coverest thyself with light as with a garment" (Psalm 104:2), so "let us . . . cast off the works of darkness, and let us put on the armour of light" (Romans 13:12). How tawdry is all else beside that! How desperately poor are all our substitutes, which so often hide sin.

"Put on thy strength," for He has strength for every emergency and every demand. When hard pressed, His strength is there. We are not told to generate it or purchase it, but *put it on!* He awaits only our appropriation.

Before going out into the arena of daily life, which so often witnesses defeat, put on the might of the risen Lord. Take hold of His strength, arm yourself with the whole armor of God. Wrap yourself around with the mail of Him who is stronger than the strong man armed. Dare to believe that in Him you are more than a match for any foe.

"The Lord is my light and my salvation; whom shall I fear? the Lord is the strength of my life; of whom shall I be afraid?" (Psalm 27:1).

We have missed all this in our day because we allow the devil to trick us into substitutes for the power of the Holy Spirit, and like Israel in Babylon, we are groveling in the dust.

But the Lord has bidden Babylon, "Come down, and sit in the dust" (Isaiah 47:1). His people are commanded to rise from the dust and sit on her throne (see Isaiah 52:2). The place of servitude was to be changed for sovereignty.

It is not too late for God to do that for us. But we need to act *now*. There must be the confession of our spiritual plight coupled with the cry for intervention from heaven that the living Lord Jesus will impart His strength to meet our weakness. This is the sure road to revival, to the deliverance of God, to Zion becoming the holy city (see Isaiah 52:1). The inner citadel of your heart is intended to be His alone: He purchased the site with His own blood; He reared the walls, and He claims it as His throne. If we yield to Him, He will yet save us, and make our lives holy even as He is holy.

There is no source of strength apart from the living Lord Jesus, so in every situation claim the power of the Holy Spirit imparted to every believer, for it is not by might, nor by power, but by His Spirit that the Christian lives to His glory. Therefore awake, and put on His strength!

The opposite to all we are by nature is in Christ, and the Holy Spirit is in us to appropriate His life in every situation. "I am unholy, but thank You, Lord, I claim Your holiness. I am ungracious, but I lay hold on Your love. When I am impatient, I draw upon your patience."

That is what it means to put on His strength: Jesus in me for everything!

5

Isaiah 52:11-15

The Church's Marching Orders

*Depart ye, depart ye, go ye out from thence, touch no unclean
thing; go ye out of the midst of her; be ye clean, that bear the
vessels of the Lord. For ye shall not go out with haste, nor go by
flight: for the Lord will go before you; and the God of Israel will
be your rereward.*

Isaiah 52:11,12

Here a great summons is sounded from heaven to the people
of God concerning their exodus from the captivity of Babylon.
The prophet is anticipating a day when God is going to lead His
people out from their bondage and captivity. Israel had raised
objections to this. They had said it could never be, for they were
too deeply entrenched in their present location and beset by
trouble. Furthermore, apparently God had forsaken and forgotten them. But He patiently and gently answers, one by one, the
objections of His people, and sums it all up in a threefold claim
in verse 1 for them to hearken, and then to awake and put on
their beautiful garments. He has stirred and startled them in
their lethargy, and demanded that there should be action.

Notice how God is pictured for us in the context: "The Lord
hath made bare his holy arm in the eyes of all the nations" (v.
10). He is pictured with His sleeves rolled up—if I may say so
reverently—ready to act, about to move in His omnipotent
power, ready to display His authority in and through the lives
of those who will obey Him.

The literal fulfilment of this prophecy is given to us in the

48

Book of Ezra, where we see the procession of God's people moving slowly, quietly, calmly, and confidently out of Babylon on a journey through the desert which took them for a period of four months across that trackless area until they reached their destination in Jerusalem. There was no fear of pursuit or recapture, because ". . . ye shall not go out with haste, nor go by flight: for the Lord will go before you; and the God of Israel will be your rereward" (v. 12). You will remember that, though they were offered military escort to protect them, they were so sure of the Lord's presence that they scorned such an idea. As they traveled so securely, the priests carried vessels in their hands which Nebuchadnezzar had taken from the temple, and which Belshazzar had used in a drunken feast—very precious vessels about which we have this word in verse 11: ". . . be ye clean, that bear the vessels of the Lord." Ezra records that there were fifty-four hundred different vessels that were to be used in the sacred worship of the temple on their return to Jerusalem.

But, of course, the significance of a passage of Scripture like this cannot possibly be limited to an immediate historic fulfillment. Only in a very limited sense did the release of the Jewish nation from Babylon fulfill the events that are recorded in prophecy. Look at the context of verse 10 again: "The Lord hath made bare his holy arm in the eyes of all the nations; and all the ends of the earth shall see the salvation of our God."

The passage which follows is perhaps the most precious chapter in the whole of the Old Testament. It speaks to us of One who was wounded for our transgressions and bruised for our iniquities, the Lord Jesus Himself. I believe there is a far greater deliverance pictured for us here than that of one nation; it is the deliverance of the whole Israel of God, the church of Jesus Christ, from captivity into which, as verse 3 says, "Ye have sold yourselves for nought; and ye shall be redeemed without money."

Isaiah is portraying here the ransom of a people who have been in a captivity far more serious, far more crushing and devastating than that of Babylon: the captivity of sin. This is a release that has been made possible by the One who was wounded for our transgressions. I believe we are moving on rapidly in history to a day when that release will be complete, and the Lord Himself will come and take His people home, and the church redeemed from every tongue and nation shall be forever with the Lord.

The force of this text, however, not only deals with the ransom of a people from Babylon, or anticipates the complete rapture and ransom of the whole body of Christ until that day when we are all taken into His presence. I would suggest to you that it is speaking about the principles of our deliverance from captivity which must be observed by the church of every age and every generation: that call to separation, to purity of life, to inward cleansing of heart, to freedom from every form of bondage. This is the sting and impact of this passage to my own soul.

It finds its expression in the New Testament in 2 Corinthians 6:17,18: "Wherefore come out from among them, and be ye separate, saith the Lord, and touch not the unclean thing; and I will receive you, And will be a Father unto you, and ye shall be my sons and daughters, saith the Lord Almighty."

The force of this passage is also expressed in Revelation 18:4, where in the final scene of world history, civilization, which is under the judgment of a holy God because of the rejection of Jesus Christ, is doomed to total destruction, and judgment is addressed, as it were, as a last opportunity by the living Lord, "Come out of her, my people, that ye be not partakers of her sins, and that ye receive not of her plagues," lest you be involved in her destruction.

If you and I complain of any divine delay that seems apparent in God's fulfillment of His Word, let me remind you of what Peter wrote: "The Lord is not slack concerning his promise, as some men count slackness; but is longsuffering to us-ward, not willing that any should perish, but that all should come to repentance" (2 Peter 3:9). I think when we get to heaven and look back on the experiences of time, we will marvel beyond all else at the patience of a holy God with His people.

I take, therefore, the words of our text as the marching orders of heaven to the church right now, and to my own soul as well as to everyone who would be delivered from the captivity of sin, and set free to know the liberty of the children of God. This is what the Lord says concerning the type of people with whom He intends to populate heaven, and I am sure we all want to be among that great company that no man can number, who "have washed their robes, and made them white in the blood of the Lamb" (Revelation 7:14).

Listen, therefore, to God's marching orders for your life, and pay heed as if your life and death depend on it, as indeed they do. For this portion of God's Word tells you that there will be clear and unmistakable evidences that are known and observed by yourself and other people which will make it clear to all that you are marching on toward Zion, that you have responded to God's briefing, and that He is releasing you from the captivity of sin. We will consider four of these evidences that stand out as we study and meditate on this chapter.

First there will be *the evidences of a constant release*. The Jew had become accustomed to Babylon after seventy years, and I suppose if you live with anything long enough you can get used to it. Custom will make anything endurable, if you stay with it long enough. Few of those alive at the end of the seventy years of captivity remembered the awful anguish, the shame and horror of that first moment when, because of their rebellion, they were transported from Jerusalem to the shame of slavery and captivity. They had conformed their life-style to the conditions in which they lived, and the majority of them had settled down quite comfortably to enjoy their captivity. I doubt whether too many of them would be overanxious to get out of it, and to exchange the comparative prosperity in Babylon for a desert march and for what they recalled of only ruins in Jerusalem. The prospect of release did not seem to attract them.

How this has burned its way into my soul! In each of our lives from time to time, if we are honest in the presence of God, there have come to us Babylons which should have no claim whatsoever upon the life of the Christian. Maybe we have forgotten the anguish, the tears, the battle of the first days of our captivity. Perhaps we have forgotten the sting of conscience when it first took place. Maybe we have almost forgotten, in an oblivion of memory, the first attempts, the failure, the reluctance with which we gave in, until at last we have almost established a comradeship with something from which in early days

we shrank in horror. Perhaps it is an amusement which fasci-
nates us now, when once we regarded it with suspicion. Or it
is a habit of life which dominates now, from which we fled with
fear of infection in early days. It may be the love of money, of
property, of things and possessions, from which once we shrank
because we knew it would catch us in its snare. Babylons such
as these have cast their fatal spell upon our soul, and against
them the voice of God speaks in urgent warning, in serious
protest, "Depart ye, depart ye, go ye out from thence."

It is a fact that a man who has accepted heaven's marching
orders for his heart and life becomes daily more sensitive to sin,
and the Spirit's voice of warning is constantly sounding in his
heart. The Christian on the attack for God knows his marching
orders: he has heard them, and dares not lay them aside. Instead
he lays aside every weight, and the sin which so easily besets
him (*see* Hebrews 12:1). His eye is on the goal, and he says,
". . . forgetting those things which are behind, and reaching
forth unto those things which are before, I press toward the
mark . . ." (Philippians 3:13,14). For the man who has responded
to his marching orders there is a perpetual exodus as, day-by-
day, he leaves self behind, and follows on to know the Lord.

It is a tremendous experience when God's alarm bell has
sounded in a man's heart, and he is on the march for the Lord
like that. May I ask you lovingly if you are on the march today,
or have you settled down in comradeship with something
against which all heaven protests? Do you survey the walls of
separation which you set up through the years, and as you look
back in memory and see them now in ruins, can you look upon
all that without a tear? God forbid! There are some people now
whom God is calling to resume their march heavenward, to step
out of Babylon and get moving, to feel again the breath of His
Holy Spirit upon their lives. His promise to the one who obeys
is, "I will receive you, And will be a Father unto you, and ye
shall be my sons and daughters" (2 Corinthians 6:17,18).

One mark, therefore, of the man who has obeyed his marching orders is that he is moving God-ward day-by-day. He is
constantly being released from captivity and satanic power, and
he is made free by the power of God with one objective and one
great goal. Is this you? Or has God spoken many times in many

places, but you have steeled your heart against His voice because you have become so tied to something or to someone
against whom heaven sounds its note of command? And you
have listened, but you have resisted, as the Spirit urges you to
depart from evil, not to be unclean, to be rid of the unholy
thing.

Are you on the march today, as a Christian? You know the
answer to that question. You know in your own heart whether
you are advancing with God, or whether you have gone back,
or got stuck in the mud somewhere.

Another evidence of the man who is accepting God's marching orders is not only the constancy of his exodus, but also *the
continuance of the calm* in his life. "... ye shall not go out with
haste, nor go by flight" (v. 12).

There are many proverbs in use which warn against the dan-
ger of rush: "More haste, less speed," and so on: but apart from
a soul really finding rest in Jesus, I do not see any hope for a
feverish life at all. Most people live at top speed, and boiling
point is never far removed. They are always in a hurry to do
everything, with their eyes glued on the clock. That feverish,
restless spirit has got into our religion at this point in time: into
our worship, our Christian service, our meditation, all with
disastrous results.

I would say the vast majority of this restless and feverish rush
on the part of Christians is due to their failure to be on the
march with God. Inner captivity of soul inevitably spells outer
restlessness in life. Failure to respond to the Lord's voice and
to step out of sin's captivity is the reason for the greatest proportion of nervous tension and breakdown which are so frequent
and common in these days. Neurotics continue to build their
castles in the air, and the psychiatrists collect the rent!

"O that thou hadst hearkened to my commandments! then
had thy peace been as a river, and thy righteousness as the
waves of the sea" (Isaiah 48:18).

People look everywhere for the source of their trouble except
to go right back to the root of it, and the fact is that God has said,
"Get out of your captivity!" and they have refused to obey.
They examine every possible cure and answer to the restless
feverishness of mind and heart and soul. They are tormented,

but refuse to examine their hearts concerning grass-root obedience to the Word of God. The tension that has so often gripped the life of the child of God, and the terrible restlessness of his life, stem right back to his disobedience.

We need to learn from the example of the Lord Jesus, through those crowded years of conflict and tension, the like of which we know nothing in our own lives, when Satan mustered everything he could against Him. Read the Gospels for yourself to confirm the statement that He moved majestically and quietly and deliberately through every onslaught and pressure, and that He had leisure for every appeal, for the touch of every weary hand, for the cry of every broken heart. There never was any trace or hint of feverishness and unrest. When others tried to hurry Him along He would say, "Your time is always ready, but My time is not yet come" (*see* John 7:6). What was His secret? It was submission to His Father's will, and this brought absolute calm into His life. That is God's purpose for you today, for Jesus said, ". . . my peace I give unto you" (John 14:27).

Consider the unrest of your own heart and life and think about it seriously. You won't find rest in religion or in any church. You will not find it in a system of doctrine. In fact, you will not find peace and rest of soul in anything or anyone apart from the living Lord Jesus Christ.

Have you laid yourself down and cast the weight of your burden on Him? If so, Isaiah 52:12 will be true, ". . . ye shall not go out with haste, nor go by flight: for the Lord will go before you; and the God of Israel will be your rereward [rearguard]."

If the Lord goes in front of you, what is the sense of trying to dash ahead? He is in front to guide, and He is also behind to guard. When you really believe this, and rest in His promise, trusting in His arrangement of your life and responding to His orders, then a wonderful sense of calm descends upon your soul. Nothing else matters in life but that. Calm is not inactivity; it is movement without friction.

If your great longing is for peace, how far do you have to look back upon life and experience until you come to the place of real peace? Ask yourself, was it disobedience to heaven's marching orders in some situation that put an end to peace? If it was, let me tell you that immediate obedience will restore it at once. The evidence of the kind of men with whom the Lord intends to populate heaven is a constant exodus from every captivity, which is followed by a calm tranquility.

Another evidence of accepting His commands is *confidence in the Lord:* ". . . for the Lord will go before you; and the God of Israel will be your rereward" (v. 12). On the occasion of the first exodus from Egypt, God guided His people by a pillar of cloud and fire, day and night. But not at this time from Babylon back to Jerusalem. There was no visible presence of God at all to guide them across the desert.

This has spoken to my heart in perhaps a strange way, as it has reminded me of early days of Christian experience, and then the years that have followed. I wonder if your heart gives an echo to that fact? Early in the Christian life the path seemed clearly defined and often we followed the steps of other mature Christians. We sat at their feet and received counsel and help. Perhaps some godly pastor helped us, who had been along the road of life for many years. There always seemed to be a crowd going on ahead, and all we had to do was follow.

Time went by and the years passed, and if we responded to heaven's marching orders the crowd thinned, until one day we find ourselves on our own. There are no footsteps on the sand ahead now. All the props have gone, and we find ourselves on our own. Indeed, other people begin to try and drink from our life, and when we suddenly recognize that this is happening, it is a terrifying moment. It is enough to make you turn and run to get in among the crowd again, unless you hear a voice saying, "Now, My child, every prop has gone from you. There is no crowd in front. You have followed My marching orders and obeyed My Word up to the light you have. You have walked on in this path of obedience, and you find yourself now alone. But I am the Way!" The Lord will go before you.

At that point there is perhaps a turning point in your Christian life. You find yourself without a single human prop, but you find yourself blessedly cast upon the Lord Himself. In the New Testament the early Christians were known as "men of the way." They had discovered the secret of blessedness, the path which would take them through every perplexity of life and present them ultimately into the very presence of God. If you were to ask them what their secret was, they would simply utter one word, "Jesus!"

In response and in obedience to His marching orders He gives us His peace, then He removes every prop, and what happens next? The man who goes through with the Lord begins to inquire from Him as to how He would react in situations. He does not ask Mr. So-and-So or Dr. Somebody-Else what he would do, but he turns directly to the Lord. When there is no footprint in the sand, thank God *He* is there. Stand still at that moment and hush every voice in His presence. Take your bearings from the Word of God, and He will give you complete confidence in Himself.

The evidences of a man who has responded to the Lord's commands are constant response and exodus, a calm in his life, and a confidence in the Lord Jesus Christ. Perhaps someone needs that word, from whose life the props have been removed in recent days, in order that you might learn to draw upon Jesus Himself.

There is another evidence of the character of the man who is seeking fully to obey the Lord, and that is *a cleansing of his heart.* Ah yes, I know that when you came to Jesus He washed away your sin. But I also know the defilement of a Christian's life that needs the constant, maintained cleansing. The second part of verse 11 says that the vessels which the priests carried were very precious, they were holy unto the Lord, and the command was, ". . . be ye clean, that bear the vessels of the Lord."

I would remind you that the men who carried them were Levites, who were set apart for this work, and possessed at least a ceremonial purity and cleansing. So, passing through the desert between Babylon and Jerusalem was a procession of holy men carrying holy vessels.

In this world in which you and I live there is also a passing procession. People do not recognize it too much, the world does not notice, but heaven watches, as it threads its way through the continents of time, bearing the holy vessels.

". . . for I know whom I have believed, and am persuaded that he is able to keep that which I have committed unto him against that day. . . . That good thing which was committed unto thee keep by the Holy Ghost which dwelleth in us" (2 Timothy 1:12,14). He is able to keep that which I have entrusted to Him, and because I have entrusted my life to Him, He has entrusted to me a sacred task, and to you, also. He has put His reputation in our hands. He has given us charge of a testimony to the truth, the announcement to the world of His way of salvation. He has put into our hands the Good News of the gospel, therefore He says to us, ". . . be ye clean, that bear the vessels of the Lord."

What manner of people ought we to be, to whom God has entrusted a task like this? How careful that the character of the glorious risen Saviour remains undimmed and unblurred by our behavior! How careful lest our testimony to the doctrine of the truth be rendered void by the life that professes it! Only the indwelling Lord Jesus can make this possible, because it is *He in me* who enables me to respond to my marching orders from heaven.

"Be ye clean. . . ." How desperately we need that cleansing today from the defilement of speech, unkindness, scandal, and gossip. How unkind can some Christian people be!

What wonderful fruit there is from a life that obeys God! It is in the setting of what has been said that some of this passage takes on a new meaning: "How beautiful upon the mountains are the feet of him that bringeth good tidings, that publisheth peace; that bringeth good tidings of good, that publisheth salvation; that saith unto Zion, Thy God reigneth!" (Isaiah 52:7). And that was the message to a people released and returning to their homeland, Zion!

There is nothing more beautiful in all the world than the life of a man set free from captivity, because what was desert when he came to it is heaven when he leaves it. You may live in a home where there is defeat and brokenness, failure and misery. Because you have obeyed God's marching orders, and are released from your own captivity, as you witness in the desert of that home, I tell you, when you leave it you will have left a bit of heaven behind you! Once there was hostility, suspicion, misunderstanding; but when there is the impact of a life that is moving on in obedience to the Lord, all that is dispelled and peace reigns.

Are you on the march with God, or have you established comradeship with something or someone against which heaven protests? Ah, that you would turn to Him today and respond to His call. He will give you the calm, the confidence, and the cleansing you require to renew fellowship with your Lord and Saviour, and make you worthy once more to be His representative in an alien world.

6

Man of Sorrows

He is despised and rejected of men; a man of sorrows, and acquainted with grief: and we hid as it were our faces from him; he was despised, and we esteemed him not.

Isaiah 53:3

A dark-skinned Ethiopian on a desert road, traveling from Jerusalem to Africa, sat in his chariot one day with the Word of God, as he possessed it then, open before him, though in fact closed to him. He was baffled and mystified, yet he longed to know the truth. He had traveled hundreds of miles on that journey from Africa to worship, but he was returning disappointed.

"Is there no key that will unlock to me the mysteries of this Book?" he would ask himself. "'. . . he is brought as a lamb to the slaughter, and as a sheep before her shearers is dumb, so he openeth not his mouth.' Of whom speaks the prophet this? of himself, or of some other man?"

As he considered this in his heart, a faithful servant of the Lord Jesus Christ came by, joined him in his chariot, and from that Scripture preached to him Jesus. He went back to his home to become the first believer in the African continent (*see* Acts 8:26-40).

Some of you may be just like that Ethiopian: although your Bible may be open, yet it is closed. These studies in the prophecy of Isaiah may have intrigued you, but you have not come to know the One of whom they speak. My prayer is that,

59

as we come to what I would call "the Holy of Holies," the veil may be rent from your mind as I would seek to do what Philip did, and preach Christ to you from this chapter.

Isaiah 53 demands several studies because Christ Himself is the only key to unlock our hearts to the tremendous treasure of truth in these verses. It is only the Lamb in the midst of the throne, the Lion of the tribe of Judah, who can claim all this to be realized in Himself. For anyone else to make such a claim would be beyond contempt. But let Jesus come near at this moment and open His heart to us, revealing His wounds. Let us see if there be any sorrow like unto His sorrow, and we realize at once that He has undisputed claim to all the depth of suffering described here.

The Saviour and His sorrow is our subject, which may sound dismal, but it most certainly is not. It is never sad to look at a battlefield when you know there has been victory. It is in that light we look back at the arena of battle, for now we know that it is a place where victory was won on our behalf. It is a very solemn subject, in a sense a sad one, but supremely a very wonderful one. It is one in which somehow we find ourselves bowed in awe in the presence of God.

". . . a man of sorrows, and acquainted with grief" (v. 3). In considering this subject let us see in it mysteries that stand out from the pages of Scripture. There is in the first place what I have called the mystery of our Lord's humiliation: ". . . he shall grow up before him as a tender plant, and as a root out of a dry ground: he hath no form nor comeliness; and when we shall see him, there is no beauty that we should desire him" (v. 2). This verse will be the basis of our next study, but I wish to introduce our subject by a consideration of it.

How different everything was from what the Jews had expected!

Their Messiah was to come with much dignity from a great and illustrious family. He was to be the Son of David, and true, He was, though He came out of that family when it was poverty-stricken. His supposed father was only a poor carpenter. He was born of a woman of humble family living in Nazareth of Galilee, a place out of which the Jews said no good thing could ever come.

Our Lord was a root out of dry ground. It was expected by
the Jews that He would make a public entry into Jerusalem in
great pomp, but instead He grew up quietly before God. He was
not observed by people; He was observed in heaven.

He grew up as a tender plant. A manger, lowly circumstances, a humble home, were His constant lot, His daily experience. His only followers were common people. Thieves were
placed on either side of Him when He was crucified. This was
utter humiliation for the Son of God.

It was expected, of course, that there would be some rare
attractiveness about Him that would draw all people to Him
and claim their hearts, but the Bible says that He had no form
or comeliness. There was nothing in His outward appearance
whatsoever to betray the fact that He was indeed God incarnate. Oh, yes, He had a beauty, but not the kind physical eyes
would appreciate. It was the beauty of holiness, the beauty of
abandonment to the will of His Father, the beauty of total
commitment to the will of God. His was the fragrance of a life
that was lived without any rival to His sovereign purpose as the
obedient Son. "Father, Thy will be done on earth as it is in
heaven," was the passion of His prayer.

Men were astonished at Him, for Isaiah 52:14 tells us that His
face was so marred more than any man, and His form more than
the sons of men. They wondered and marveled at the treatment
He received when He hid not His face from shame and spitting.

Not only did our wonderful Lord divest Himself of all the
glory that was due to Him from before the foundation of the
world, all the majesty and worth and worship of heaven, but He
submitted Himself to the disgraces and shame that were due
only to the most despised of men.

So He humbled Himself. He who was absolutely radiant with
all the beauty and glory of heaven stooped to the depths of
humiliation that He might lift the vilest of humanity back into
the presence of God.

What condescension that He who became man—the One
who created the oceans and rivers—should stoop to ask the
favor of a drink from a woman who was a harlot! That He lived
in daily contact with sinners: constantly surrounded by the
worst, the most miserable and sinful of all: that He should be

obedient to death, even the death of the cross, and suffer this at the hand of men—this is His humiliation.

I want to pause to emphasize something at this point. These days it appears that we must dress up the gospel to make it attractive. We have to use methods of technique which must be smart, well-presented, streamlined. There must be something about the presentation of the gospel that will appeal to people, and so hours are dissipated in thinking out methods of approach that will appeal to what is called "the modern mind." I wonder if we stop to think that in our efforts to make the gospel message "attractive" we are drawing the curtain across the face of Jesus in His humiliation? The only one who can make Him attractive to people is the Holy Spirit. Man cannot do it by any methods of preaching he might try, or by any program or technique. Only the Holy Spirit can make the Lord Jesus so real and vital that people will fall in love with Him and worship Him, and it is the delight of God the Holy Spirit to point to the humiliation of God the Son.

He suffered that for me. He stooped to this to save my soul. He was humiliated like this in order that He might redeem me, and that none might ever be lower than He was.

The gospel needs no attractiveness added to it. He who makes the appeal to the attractiveness of Jesus, the Spirit of God, is the One who points us to the shame and spitting, to the scorn and buffeting, and to the form that was marred more than the sons of men. It is the Holy Spirit who makes His cross so attractive, and the beauty of the holiness of His life so wonderful that somehow, as to a magnet, in recognition of personal need, the soul is drawn to an experience of the saving power of Jesus —not by our techniques, but by Holy Spirit conviction.

Here, too, is the mystery of His sorrow: "He is despised and rejected of men; a man of sorrows, and acquainted with grief" (v. 3).

What a name to give to Jesus! We might have called Him a Man of holiness, because He was without sin. We might have said He was a Man of eloquence, because "Never man spake like this man" (John 7:46), the people said. We might have called Him a Man of love, for love never shone out of any life as it did out of the life of Jesus. Yet we gaze upon Christ, and know that the most significant, unique, and wonderful thing about Him was His sorrow. You see it on His face. You see it as He wept over Jerusalem and at the grave of Lazarus.

We never read in the Bible that Jesus laughed. It would make a very interesting study to consider the laughter of God as recorded in His Word. It is reserved for His derision concerning the wicked: "He that sitteth in the heavens shall laugh: the Lord shall have them in derision" (Psalm 2:4). This is the laughter of an omnipotent God in absolute authority over all the sin of mankind. But it is not written that Jesus laughed. Yes, I know there is the joy of the Lord; I know that the writer to the Hebrews says that He, for the joy that was set before Him, despised the cross, enduring the shame. But the impression conveyed about our Lord Jesus is that He is a man of sorrows.

Have you ever stopped to ask yourself what sorrow really is? What is its root? What is the deepest thing about sorrow? It is not simply personal loss, tragic though that is. Basically that kind of sorrow grieves because it has done something to *me* and hurt *me*. There is, of course, no element of selfishness in true sorrow. I believe that the deepest thing about sorrow is its end result in love that can be experienced for another; the deep concern for a person who, when threatened with disaster, rejects what love desires to do for him.

Pause to think of the sorrow of Jesus. Love incarnate is revealed in Him. And He sees the object of His love, namely the human heart, eluding His grasp, turning cold toward Him, poisoned by misunderstanding of His mission and of His aim. He finds a refusal to accept His salvation, a complete rejection of His claims. He is a man of sorrows.

He came to earth with a message of love and redemption, but all the names of contempt that men could think of were heaped upon Him. They said He was drunk, that He had a devil and was demon-possessed; they charged Him with every crime that their malice could conceive. Yet His sorrow was not because people slighted Him, but because in doing so they were committing spiritual suicide. He is a man of sorrows with a pang in His heart over a soul that rejects His claim, and in rejecting it casts himself automatically into outer darkness.

"O Jerusalem, Jerusalem . . . how often would I have gathered

thy children together, even as a hen gathereth her chickens
under her wings, and ye would not!" (Matthew 23:37). Yes, He
is a Man of Sorrows, not grieving primarily because He had
been hurt, but because His purpose was being rejected, and by
that rejection men were casting themselves into hell.

In the crowning sorrow of His life there came upon Him the
chastisement which procured our peace (*see* Isaiah 53:5), as He
wrestled in a garden until the sweat stood out from every pore
in His body, and His soul was exceeding sorrowful, even unto
death.

Stop now, and ask if you have ever added to the sorrow of the
Man of Sorrows. I wonder if we have caused His heart to be sad
because we have not appreciated His love. It was not only in the
first century, but it is today that He comes to His own—yes, to
His own, to people who have been redeemed by His blood, His
children—to find they have barred the door. How many times
has Jesus wanted to talk with you, friend, early in the morning?
He was there to meet you, but you missed the appointment. He
has come to the garden of your life to find fruit, but, alas, He
has found it barren. He came that He might have fellowship and
communion, but you were too busy. You failed to listen to Him.
As He came to your soul He found the wall of separation in
ruins, a life that was barren, and instead of a welcome He
received a rebuff.

Perhaps as you look back over this week you find you have
driven another nail into His hands, or a sword into His side; you
have made Him sorrowful. You have not given Him that which
He desires, the adoration and worship of your heart. He is truly
a Man of Sorrows.

Think now of this in its other aspect. Paul, giving his testimony in writing to the church at Philippi, says his great ambi-
tion was that "I may know him, and the power of his resurrection, and the fellowship of his sufferings" (Philippians 3:10). Yes,
he says, I want to enter into something of what the Man of
Sorrows suffered over a Christ-rejecting world. That is why
Paul, writing to the church at Galatia, says, "My little children,
of whom I travail in birth again until Christ be formed in you"
(Galatians 4:19).

The fellowship of His sufferings: have I entered into that?

have you? As a Christian, do you care? You will not be long in Christian experience before you come to see that if you stand for truth and holiness, for God and His Word, and you shun not to declare the whole counsel of God, something will happen in your life. Some will bless you and some will blast you, but nobody will be indifferent to you. Preach the sovereignty of the Lord, preach the cross, the crucified life, and the absolute totalitarian demand of a risen Christ for all there is of His child; preach the life which accepts no possible rival except to do God's will, and I tell you everyone within the sound of your testimony, or the sound of your message, will immediately come right off the fence of neutrality and land on one side or the other. If you are like me, when those who seem to get off the fence on the wrong side resist and begin to blaspheme and get mad—then you know what your reaction is. The reaction of a man of God should not be sorrowful because such people hurt him, for they don't. It is to be sorrowful in the rejection of the voice of the preacher, of the Sunday-school teacher, of any Christian leader, for the rejection of that voice is not the casting off of the individual but the rejection of the voice of God. I pray more and more in my life and ministry (and I trust you do, too) that the Lord will help me to enter into what it means to share in the fellowship of His suffering, for here is the mystery of His sorrow, the bleeding heart that wept over those who in rejecting Him were rejecting their only hope of life.

Get into the presence of God sometime today, on your own, and ask how much of that you have felt over a soul that has turned away from God. Paul says, "I travail in birth . . . until Christ be formed in you" (Galatians 4:19). My deep concern is to remember that men and women will only be born into the kingdom when a Christian enters into heart-travail for them.

Consider finally what I have called the mystery of pain: "But he was wounded for our transgressions, he was bruised for our iniquities: the chastisement of our peace was upon him; and with his stripes we are healed" (v. 5).

Wounded, bruised, chastised: what does that mean? Immediately your thoughts go to the soldiers as they spat in His face, to the scourge that plowed great weals across His back. Your mind will go perhaps more than all to the cry on the cross, "My

God, my God, why hast thou forsaken me?"

Have you ever struggled with Hebrews 5:7? I have to acknowledge it has been a problem to me. ". . . in the days of his flesh, when he had offered up prayers and supplications with strong crying and tears unto him that was able to save him from death, and was heard in that he feared."

What does it mean? Can it be that our Lord was so torn with pain and suffering that He was afraid He would die in the Garden before He reached the cross and paid the price of our sin? Could it be that the pressure of physical pain was so unendurable that there was every fear in His mind that He would collapse before His purpose of salvation was accomplished? Therefore He poured out prayer and supplication with crying and tears unto Him that was able to save Him from death at that moment, and He was heard in that He feared. If the anticipation of the cross wrung His heart like that, I wonder what enduring it must have meant to Him. Recall how He was treated before the judgment seat when the soldiers almost murdered Him with their scourging, and then how they nailed Him to the tree. We can think of all this, but I do not think I have even yet touched the very depths of these words.

I think about the Lord Jesus praying, "Oh, Father, I cannot die now. It must be only on a tree, only outside the city wall, only where the price must be paid that men might be saved. I cannot die; I cannot allow this physical frame to be crushed to death by the brutality of men. This can only happen on the cross." And therefore He was strengthened.

Still I have not touched the depths. I believe that the deepest pain of all, the heart of all His sorrow, the reason for His name, a Man of Sorrows, was because the deepest scourge, the severest grief, the worst pain, and the most awful agony did not come from men, but from God. Not from without but from within. For it was the hand of a holy God that bruised Him, and it was the iron rod of heaven's justice that broke Him. And a wrath which no man can ever know—the wrath of a holy God against all sin—spent and exhausted itself. For "it pleased the Lord to bruise him: he hath put him to grief" (Isaiah 53:10). The fact that your sin and mine was laid upon Him—that this perfect, sensitive, holy, pure nature, so sensitive as a quickening, quivering wound—that *that* nature was identified with all the filth and corruption, the shame and beastliness of human sin, is the deepest pain of all. And God inflicted it.

What kind of pain, therefore, is God going to inflict one day upon the man who rejects His Son Jesus Christ? What will be the suffering in hell for the person who has heard of the Saviour, but rejected and rebelled against Him, when God did that to His Son to make salvation possible?

I ask you in deep love and concern and prayer, what will you have to endure at the judgment seat of Christ if you have trifled with the things that drove Him to Calvary? What if repentance has not been real? What if forsaking from sin has not been genuine on your part? What if your turning to God has only been mere profession? What if you have gone through life as a professing Christian, allowing this and that in your life to take the place of preeminence, in the light of the fact that the depth and mystery of all pain was that the hand of a holy God fell upon His Son at Calvary? As you think seriously about all this, surely your desire is to fly to the wounded side of the Saviour, and plead His mercy, His forgiveness, His patience and redemption.

7

Principles of Growth

For he shall grow up before him as a tender plant, and as a root out of a dry ground: he hath no form nor comeliness; and when we shall see him, there is no beauty that we should desire him.

Isaiah 53:2

When you read a chapter like this, and also other similar passages in the Old Testament, are you not surprised that the Jews could ever mistake their Messiah when He came? But they did: they were looking for someone with some outward material splendor. All the passages in Scripture which had so clearly pointed the way to a Man of sorrows, God's Lamb, slain from before the foundation of the world, somehow failed to dawn upon their minds.

Yet when you think again, it is not so strange, because it is just the same today. Though the message of the gospel is so basically simple, yet sometimes the greatest intellect cannot understand it, for the fact is, whether a man is a Jew or a Gentile, sin has rendered him mentally incapacitated. He cannot by himself discern the things of the Spirit (*see* 1 Corinthians 2:14). They need revelation. As we turn, therefore, to this precious portion of God's Word, how we need to pray and to thank the Lord that His Holy Spirit is with us to reveal these wonderful truths to our hearts, as only He can.

In thinking about the strength of the Lord Jesus, about the principles of His growth, we contemplate something which is not merely applicable to Him, but which is applicable to you and me in our daily lives. If I would understand how to grow in the things of God and understand the real secret of strength for my life and ministry, then I have set before me a pattern of the Saviour.

"He shall grow up as a tender plant." Turn that over in your mind. What a tender plant He was! How weak He was! There was a manger in Bethlehem; a flight into another country to escape the wrath of King Herod; a life of obscurity in a carpenter's shop. There was no apparent publicity, no program, no pomp or show. At any moment it would seem as if our Lord could indeed have been destroyed, He seemed so vulnerable. In fact, when the day came that He hung upon a cross, one would imagine that He had indeed been destroyed. But three days later He rose again, ascended into heaven, and imparted to all His followers a power by which they were able to rock the world.

It was this "tender plant" who learned the principle of spiritual growth, as He learned it in the school of obedience, who one day was crucified, arose from the tomb, and ascended into heaven. It was this "tender plant," having learned, I say, God's principles of growth, who won the right for all who follow Him to share this same power, this same revolutionary gospel, this same dynamic message which is able to shatter the power of sin and death over mankind.

Though it would seem in some quarters that Christianity might appear to have lost its influence, I would say without hesitation or fear of contradiction that wherever these principles of growth which Jesus Christ followed are applied in a life, there is the same impact, the same authority and power. But when the church or the Christian moves away to other means of spiritual progress, they have sacrificed all authority.

What were these principles in the life of the Lord Jesus?

"As a root out of a dry ground." I want you to think with me about this phrase as we apply it to His life. Perhaps some of you love gardening—I don't personally, but maybe you do!—and you spend much time working there. You cultivate and prepare the ground, plant, hoe, and water. No wonder when summer comes you have lovely flowers. You have given so much time to the cultivation of the soil that it would be a tragedy, almost an impossibility, if flowers failed to be produced. They owe everything to the richness of the soil with which you worked.

But the Lord Jesus grew up as a root out of dry ground. In other words, He did not owe anything to the surroundings in which He lived: He owed nothing to the soil. He imparted everything to it, and received nothing from it. Think about this in terms of His life, first with regard to His natural descent. He came of the tribe of Judah, we read, but the glory had departed. He received nothing because of heredity, nor did He owe a single thing to it. He owed nothing to the nation in which He was born. It was morally, religiously, spiritually dead. The scribes and Pharisees, the religious leaders of His time, were spending their time with all the intricacies of interpreting the law, and were absolutely insensible to the reality of their Saviour. The Lord Jesus came into a situation like that, owing nothing to His background, His birth, or His inheritance.

Then He owed nothing to the people whom He chose to be His disciples. It would have been wonderfully possible for our Lord to have chosen some great intellect, some key personality, to have found such a person and won him to Himself. He could have gone to Rome or Athens and found some very clever men; He could have used some very brilliant scholars to propagate the gospel, but He did not do that. Instead He found some rough, dirty fishermen. That is what they were! And from that rugged background He took a little group of men in order that they might propagate the truth. He did not owe one thing to His disciples. He made them. Everything they became for Him, He made them.

He owed nothing to His followers nor to the way He used to spread His message. You will recall that He refused military aid: He refused to use the sword. He did not use any material power. I do not find Him advocating to His disciples the attraction of the concert hall in order to build up the kingdom of heaven. The gospel was to disdain every bit of Saul's armor. It had no flash method whatsoever to propagate the truth. It was to stand entirely in its own strength. It was a root out of dry ground.

Jesus Christ owed nothing to the means He used for proclaiming His message. It was not to be a religion of show, but of discipline, of crucifixion, of surrender and commitment, and these were the things that would make it dynamic.

Further, the Lord owed nothing to the times in which He lived. Some people say that the conditions were absolutely ideal for the birth of the Christian faith. I would deny that wholeheartedly. They were completely and utterly against any possibility, apart from a miracle, of the new, vital faith breaking out and breaking loose. It was an age of luxury, vice, and self-indulgence. Civilization then, as now, was rotten to the core; vice abounded everywhere. Jesus Christ owed nothing to His surroundings.

I would go on to say that He owed nothing to human nature, that is to people like us. Mankind has never been an ally of His message. Human nature has always been antagonistic to the message of the gospel. The Word of the Lord says, "Crucify the flesh!" "Believe, not understand." "Commit, not analyze." "Love your enemies, do good to them that despitefully use you." It cuts completely across all the natural instincts of the human heart. It provides nothing for pride, for sensuality, for passion, for sin. It cuts all that down completely.

The Lord Jesus was, then, a root out of dry ground, owing nothing to anything around Him, to people, circumstances, plans, programs, propaganda. He was a root out of dry ground, and this was the pattern He followed, the principle of His growth.

I deliberately left out two words which are the key to this verse in order that we might be impressed with the background of the life of the Lord Jesus. What was the secret of His strength? Now get this, for it is the principle for our own lives, for the life of our churches, and for the spread of the gospel today: owing nothing to any situation around us, to no ally, propaganda, program, nothing of this kind. The church is as a root out of dry ground. So what was the secret of the Lord's strength? Read the verse again, "For he shall grow up *before him* as a tender plant. . . ." Recall also the Gospel of Luke 2:40 which says concerning Jesus, ". . . the child grew, and waxed strong in spirit, filled with wisdom: and the grace of God was upon him."

In other words, here is the Saviour owing nothing to and receiving nothing from any environment or friends, heredity or other influences. He is growing up as a root out of dry ground, and He is growing up before the Lord. He is growing from innocence to holiness without any aid at all around Him, owing nothing to His descent, to human nature, to His followers. The world does not notice that kind of growth, but heaven did, and watched God's perfect Man fulfilling the great purpose of the glory of God that in His life He might grow and mature, because He was growing before the Lord.

What does this mean? I believe it means that, as heaven watched Him grow, God's perfect Man was revealed growing before the Lord with an undivided affection, for He loved the Lord His God with all His might, with all His soul, and with all His strength.

It meant, too, that He had an undivided will. He said, "I do always [not sometimes] those things that please him" (John 8:29). He learned obedience through the things that He suffered (see Hebrews 5:8). His will was never opposed to the will of His Father, as He lived totally adjusted and yielded to that will which was good and perfect. Because He had an undivided affection with an unopposing will, constantly pliable and yielded to the authority of heaven, Jesus was God's perfect Man with an intelligence and understanding and a grip upon any situation. He had an unclouded intelligence, because He grew up before the Lord in a perfect and unbroken communion with God His Father.

Because He has walked the path of submission, the Lord Jesus is able to reveal to men the way of life, of redemption, and of deliverance. He has now come to establish in this sinful, wicked world of ours a principle of living, not only for Himself but for each of us, until one day, blessed be His name, He comes again to take to be with Himself those who have accepted this principle of life—men and women who have received His life into their hearts at their new birth by the indwelling Holy Spirit, and are beginning to live their lives on this identical principle of growth. Here then is a power that Jesus releases to human hearts that causes them to grow as He grew before the Lord.

If you were to read church history you would find that when the church followed this principle of growth she has been irresistible. When she has forsaken it for her own way, her own devices and methods, she has been completely beaten. In New Testament days, or soon thereafter, the great colossus of Rome was unable to stand against the authority of the gospel of Jesus Christ. True, very often the church bowed before the storm of opposition, but she has never been broken by it. To this day in China, in Russia, in other lands ruled by atheistic materialism, where you find a little group of Christians who are irresistible and invincible, it is because their lives have been gripped by this principle of growth. They grow before the Lord with an undivided will, with an unbroken affection, and therefore with a deep experience of understanding and communion with the Lord Jesus Christ. Perhaps they are not recognized by the world at large, because they are just a root out of dry ground.

Let this matter become far more personal as you think about the whole question of growth and the strength of the Lord Jesus. Reflect on your own spiritual life. When Jesus comes to you, what sort of soil does He find in your heart? Is it fertile soil in which the seed of His life grows readily and easily? Personally, I don't find it that way. It took a tremendous hammerblow of the Word of God upon my heart to break it, for I did not find that repentance came to me naturally. I did not find that faith in Jesus Christ was something easy and simple, something that I could achieve.

None of these transforming changes come by nature. If they come at all, it is because the Holy Spirit reveals Christ to our hearts, and the whole experience of conversion is as a root out of dry ground.

When Jesus stepped across the threshold of your life, what dry ground He found, didn't He? But has it been any different since? As He lives in your heart day-by-day, does He find an ally there? If the grace of the Lord Jesus is really triumphing, is it because He found something in you that helped Him to win through or not? I can only bear witness to this, that the grace of God in my life has triumphed when I have been driest, when my life has been weakest, and when I have been conscious in my own heart of being utterly and completely unworthy of His salvation. When I have been conscious of the barrenness of the soil of my heart, it is then, blessed be God, that the grace and power of His Holy Spirit has entered to overcome that barrenness. How He loves to take just a dry piece of soil and flood it with His presence! Perhaps you are conscious of that very thing. You look up into the face of the Master and say, "Lord Jesus, my life is so barren, I am not worthy to serve You." Praise Him that barrenness is no reason for failing to serve Him. The only reason for such failure is a sense of your fitness for service. Pride hinders the working of the Holy Spirit, because the human spirit has never bowed before His omnipotence.

If you are feeling like a bit of dry ground, with a life that is barren and empty, and so futile that you are crying out, "I could never grow!" then remember the Lord Jesus came as a root out of dry ground, and you are to grow into Him. Accept these principles of growth, receive His life into your heart, and watch what He can do when He gets possession of that patch of dry soil that is you. Ask Him now to come into this dryness and make it fruitful, to pour floods of Holy Spirit life upon it until the power of Christ rests upon you.

Now, of course, this is going to take discipline. What does that mean? I believe it means giving Jesus your mind, your full attention. Have you ever stopped to ask yourself how many minutes you have in a day? Well, the average day contains 960 minutes. How many of those do you spend thinking about Jesus, growing up unto Him? You cannot include the minutes of your personal quiet time, because you would have to exclude the time you spend wandering around, woolgathering, thinking about other things. So how many minutes do you give? Suppose an angel stepped down before you now and said, "You have spent an average of six minutes a day in the last week thinking about your Saviour," would that shock you?

It has been estimated that in an average life-span of seventy-five years, a Christian will spend twenty-three years asleep, nineteen years at work, six years in traveling, seven and one-half years in dressing and attending to personal toilet, nine years with TV and other forms of entertainment, six years eating, four years of sickness—and one-half year in devotions. You can test the truth of this by just contemplating how you yourself spend only one week of your time, and you will find out—maybe to your great humiliation—that these figures bear a strong resemblance to the truth.

Are we really growing up into Him? You cannot learn anything without concentration. Language study, music, any quest for knowledge demands time, and it is impossible to grow up before God by spending a few skimped minutes each day with Him. There is discipline in this, and it means giving Jesus your mind, and if He has that, then the mind of Christ begins to be imparted to you. This is the principle of Christian growth by which the believer matures in Christ.

This is not popular teaching in the church in many areas these days. The average church member does not like growing up into the Lord. He wants to owe something to some outside cause. He wants to use other things to assist in making the gospel of the Lord Jesus attractive, so he forsakes this principle of growth, and in doing that he forsakes the only means by which he can receive the power, authority, and anointing of the Holy Spirit. If the Christian would grow up before God, then He promises that He will give the blessing and power of His Holy Spirit.

Growth is synonymous with cross-bearing, and the cross of Christ is the symbol of death. It stands for the abrupt, violent end of a human being. The man in Roman times who took up his cross and started down the road had already said good-bye to his friends. He was not coming back. He was not going out to have his life redirected; he was going out to have it ended. In coming to Christ we do not bring our old life on to a higher plane; we leave it at the cross, for the corn of wheat must fall into the ground and die (*see* John 12:24). This is the discipline of growth and the only way by which the child of God can be transformed into the image of his Lord and Saviour, Jesus Christ. God saves a man, not by improving his old life, but by crucifying it, and by raising him up to walk in newness of life in Christ (*see* Galatians 2:20).

Are you willing to present your barrenness to the Lord, accept His discipline, and experience the floods of life and power that He can pour into the utterly yielded soil of your heart?

8

The Heart of Christianity

But he was wounded for our transgressions, he was bruised for our iniquities: the chastisement of our peace was upon him; and with his stripes we are healed.

Isaiah 53:5

In these wonderful words is revealed to us the great conception in the mind of God concerning the nature of sin. The gospel goes to the heart of human need and the cross, of course, is at the very heart of the gospel. We have to see how God deals with sin and what is the effect upon the individual who accepts the treatment.

"He was wounded for our transgressions," and the word means disobedience.

"He was bruised for our iniquities," and that word means defilement, the downward drag of our human nature.

"The chastisement of our peace was upon him; and with his stripes we are healed."

First consider the character of sin as it is revealed here, and notice that God in His mercy—I say, in His *mercy*—treats sin as a disease: "With his stripes we are healed." Through the suffering of our Saviour our sin is pardoned. It is regarded here as the healing of a deadly sickness. If God were to deal with sin right now as sin, and summon each person to answer for it immediately, we would be without hope, for no one can defend himself against the accusation of a holy God.

So for this present time He deals with men as suffering from

76

a disease which can be cured, rather than as living in a state of rebellion which must be punished. I want you to grasp that. In this life God deals with us, not as rebels, but as people who are sick, desperately sick at heart, but it is a disease which He can cure. One day, if it is not cured, we face Him as rebels.

Now this is part of the wonderful grace of God that, while sin is a disease, it is much more than a disease. If our failures, iniquities, were merely the result of some unavoidable sickness, if we are what we are because we are hopelessly diseased, then we might claim pity. But that is not the whole story, because we sin willfully. We deliberately choose evil. We transgress in heart, and our sin is not a calamity but a crime. Yet God in mercy looks upon it in this life in such a way as to give us hope. He looks not so much at the wickedness of sin as the sickness of sin, and deals with it as a spiritual complaint of the worst possible kind. Consider sin in that way, remembering that you and I will never avail ourselves of the remedy of God's grace until we have accepted His diagnosis of our real trouble, sin.

Sin was no part of human nature when God created man. When the first man, Adam, was living in the original intention of God, he had a crown of glory on his head: he was truly man, created in the image of God. But from the moment of his rebellion he became the victim of a dreadful disease which, if it is not cured, will ultimately destroy him like a cancerous growth entering his heart. Immediately the crown of his manhood fell from him. The light went out of his mind, and he was unable to think aright; the joy went out of his heart, and he lost his happiness.

Sin is the source of every trouble that besets the human race, for it has put the whole system out of order. It puts the individual right off center, and causes the body to rule his judgment instead of his judgment ruling his body. Putting it very simply, a man is intended to ride the horse, but because of sin the horse rides the man!

This dreadful disease has driven man completely away from the center of God's purpose. It is the animal in the individual life that crushes the mental, physical, and spiritual life, and every faculty of the human personality is thrown out of gear. Man's equilibrium is disturbed because of sin, and he who once

wore the glory of his manhood and was created in the image of
a holy God has become bruised, marred, sick, broken, his conscience ruined, his understanding faulty, his will enfeebled, and
the principle of integrity and the resolve to do right completely
undermined.

". . . when we were yet without strength, in due time Christ
died for the ungodly" (Romans 5:6). And it is sin which has
reduced mankind to this state. As a disease, it has deadened all
sensibility. Cancer can eat away at the human body undetected,
and the more sinful a man becomes, the less he is conscious of
being a sinner; the deeper he is in the mire, the more slow he
is to recognize his trouble. Like a man who has become a victim
to drugs, and can take greater and greater doses until what
would kill a hundred people has no effect upon him, so sin has
stupified the individual life, and as a disease it pollutes and
makes a man utterly impure.

So it is that the Lord has prepared a place—terrifying thought
—where the man who is finally unclean and refuses God's
remedy will eternally be shut up, because justice must keep out
of heaven anything that would defile.

Think how sin injures a man. It makes communion with God
impossible. It deprives him of all spiritual sensitiveness, all possibility of spiritual hearing or feeling. It removes every spiritual
appetite, and ultimately it proves fatal, for sin when it is finished
brings forth death.

Maybe you know in your heart, as I speak to you from experience, that sin is the death of peace. It is the end of all joy; it
destroys all hope, and apart from an intervention from heaven,
sin grows worse and worse, not merely in this life, but in an
eternity of separation from God. This I understand to be what
the New Testament has to say about the eternal punishment of
the unbeliever. A dreadful doctrine from which many people
shrink with a sense of repulsion, but one which stands in the
Bible, and therefore which we must face: hell, the separation of
the unrepentant, sinful man from God. If you say, "Well, that
won't disturb him too much, because he has lived apart from
God in this life," there is the tremendous distinction that in this
world he has been able to purchase that which, in some degree
at least, satisfied his appetites. In hell he has nothing. Evil men

grow worse and worse through all eternity.

Yes, God deals with sin as a disease, and I want you to feel it to be this—a contagious, defiling, mortal sickness which made Isaiah cry out "From the sole of the foot even unto the head there is no soundness in it; but wounds, and bruises, and putrifying sores" (Isaiah 1:6).

Why do I say all this? Why, as I speak about the cross, do I spend time talking about these things?

A group of engineers were once meeting together around a drawing board laying out the plans for an immense new bridge over a very large river. As they conferred and discussed it together, one man kept raising one difficulty after another, until his colleagues became impatient. "Why do you keep on raising these problems?" they asked. "Gentlemen," he replied, "I raise them in order that I might solve them."

It is against the background of this deadly, foul, corrupting disease of sin that I present to you the glorious fact that "with his stripes we are healed."

I hope therefore I have laid before you the real character of sin, what it is and what it has done to your life. Nobody accepts the gospel of the grace of God until he sees this, admits it, confesses it, and loathes it, crying out to God for deliverance from it.

What is the cure the Lord provides? Here we step on holy ground. "He was wounded for our transgressions, he was bruised for our iniquities . . . and with his stripes we are healed."

The breathtaking record (if we were not so used to it) is that God sent His only begotten Son into this world to take upon Himself our nature in order that we might be delivered. It is recorded in the Bible how He lived as a man among other men, and after more than thirty years, in which He was tested in all points like we are, yet without sin, and in which He was proved to be utterly sinless, at the conclusion of His life came the commendation from heaven, "This is my beloved Son, in whom I am well pleased" (Matthew 17:5). He went to Gethsemane to drink the cup that His Father had given Him. He went into Pilate's hall and before Herod's judgment seat, and finally He went up the hill Golgotha where He died the Just for the unjust —by His stripes we are healed.

I pause to talk to you about the stripes of Jesus, although I confess a sense of utter inability. They were inflicted on His body and on His soul, for His whole person was made a sacrifice for us. As to His body, such was the agony of our Lord that, you recall, He sweated drops of blood. Before Pilate and before Herod He was scourged, spat upon, and buffeted; they put a crown of thorns upon His head. The scourge that they used was made of the tough hide of an ox, twisted into knots into which were inserted hard animal bone. Every time it fell upon His sacred back, as Psalm 129:3 records, "The plowers plowed upon my back: they made long their furrows." Our Lord was spared no kind of pain. At Calvary they kicked Him and threw Him on the ground. They nailed Him to a cross of wood, raised Him up upon it and dropped it into the socket with His body hanging there until it was said of Him, "I am poured out like water, and all my bones are out of joint: my heart is like wax; it is melted in the midst of my bowels. My strength is dried up like a potsherd; and my tongue cleaveth to my jaws; and thou hast brought me into the dust of death" (Psalm 22:14,15).

There our dear Lord hung, a spectacle to God and man, while Jews and Romans gloated over Him until He cried, "It is finished!" And having drunk that cup to its last drop, He gave up the ghost. With holy majesty He dismissed His spirit into the hands of His Father (see John 19:28-30).

His bodily suffering was nothing compared with the suffering of His soul. "My soul," He said to His disciples, "is exceeding sorrowful, even unto death" (Matthew 26:38). Betrayed by Judas, deserted by His disciples, these were just the beginnings, because the real pressure upon the heart and soul of Jesus, the essence and substance of all His grief, was that He was wounded *for* our transgressions and bruised *for* our iniquities.

It was the load of sin that He bore that was focused upon Him in that tremendous transaction in which God the Father, God the Son, and God the Holy Spirit participated for the redemption of men who, from the crown of the head to the sole of the foot, are full of putrifying sores. That was the worst agony of all. When His Father turned His back upon the One who was made sin for us, our great and wonderful Substitute, the Lord Jesus cried, "My God, my God, why hast thou forsaken me?" He suffered a horror of anguish instead of a horror of hell into which you and I would have been flung had He not paid the price.

"Cursed is every one that hangeth on a tree" (Galatians 3:13). I do not know that I understand what that means, but I do know it is the limit of suffering. Beloved, these stripes were for us, and the remedy for our disease is found in them, and in them alone.

If you are still saying, "Is there anything I can do to remove the guilt of sin?" I say to you, "Nothing. By His stripes we are healed, and He has not left one stripe for you to bear."

"But," you may ask, "must I not believe on Him?"

Yes, indeed, you must, but faith does not heal you. It is by His stripes that you are healed. Faith applies the healing to the wound of sin.

"So I must repent of sin," you say.

Surely you must. Repentance is the sign of healing, but the stripes of Jesus heal you, not your own repentance. Those stripes when they are applied to your heart work repentance in you, and so you begin to hate sin and to love the One who died for you.

For our salvation we must rely upon one thing only, and that is the wounds of Jesus, nothing else, trusting in Him as the One who has suffered on our behalf: I know that a holy God cannot punish me for the offence whose punishment has already been borne by my Saviour. If He has borne my guilt, then, bless His name, I won't have to bear it. I have been condemned to death for my sin, but Christ has died in my place, therefore there is now no condemnation for me to bear. That is the ground of assurance for the person who has come to Jesus: he lives because Jesus died. He is accepted before God because the Saviour was accepted. He is clear of all guilt, and none can touch him. He that believes on Him is not condemned, for by His stripes we are healed. That is God's wonderful provision.

Now look further. What is the consequence of accepting God's provision for sin? "With His stripes we are healed." What does that mean? It means that when, by faith, I apply the remedy, when I take my stand beneath the cross of Jesus and can say, "My faith looks up to Thee, Thou Lamb of Calvary," the moment I accept the remedy it becomes effective in my life.

Some say that if such a message is preached it makes people careless about the way they live. Not at all. The very worst men become the very best men by trusting in Jesus and receiving His life to indwell them. You see, His healing is so thorough. It means in the first place that character is healed. The drunkard becomes sober, the violent man becomes gentle, the liar becomes truthful, the impure become holy, the proud become humble. This is the outcome of applying the remedy, and believe me, if grace does not do that for me it is worthless. The Lord Jesus Himself said, "... by their fruits ye shall know them" (Matthew 7:20). If the fruit is not changed, then the tree is not changed. If the character is not Christlike, then the soul is not saved.

The Saviour has healed us of our transgressions—our disobedience. He has healed us of our iniquity—the downward pull of the old nature. The atonement of Jesus Christ when it is applied—not to the intellect or the mind—to the *heart*, heals the disease of sin. He who believes in Jesus is sanctified as well as justified, and by faith becomes a totally different kind of person, for "if any man be in Christ, he is a new creature: old things are passed away; behold, all things are become new" (2 Corinthians 5:17). Yes, the effect of applying the remedy and looking off to the wounds of Jesus is immediate.

There is something else. When a man trusts that remedy his conscience is healed. How sin crushes him! See him walking along the road, trying to be a good Christian. He is putting up quite a performance of being religious, but look at his face. There is no joy in it. He is under a cloud, burdened, spiritless, joyless, unhappy. But when he comes really to trust the Lord, see the change in his face! His very countenance is altered. Why, the cloud has gone, and his face is lit up with the glow of the presence of Jesus Christ! Yes, his conscience is healed when he looks at the wounds of Jesus.

And something even more wonderful: a man's personality is put back on center. His judgment is healed, his affections are changed, and now, instead of the body controlling his judgment, it is operating in reverse. Now, because of the indwelling of the Spirit, the judgment of that man is back where it should be and is controlling the body. Sin is no longer loved, but God is loved, and the great desire of the man's heart is to be like the Lord Jesus. The whole man has been healed, his whole life has been changed. With His stripes we are healed.

That is the gospel. But I must say one further word in conclusion: you are either healed or you are not. You are either made new by grace, or you are still in the sickness of sin. Please ask yourself this question: Where are you? You must know. You may not know the date of your conversion, but that does not matter. You may forget the date of your birthday sometime, but that does not mean you are not alive. The point is this, do you trust the Lord Jesus? Has that trust made you a new person? Has that confidence in Christ given you peace, the assurance of sin being forgiven? Has that forgiveness made you love Him, and out of that love is it your delight to obey the Lord? Then you are healed. You are His child, and you belong to Him.

However, if you are not healed, then why aren't you? If you know the gospel then why don't you receive it? You say, "I can't see this thing that you are talking about, I just can't understand it."

Here is a lady sewing a button on her husband's coat. As she is doing so, she suddenly looks up and says, "You know, the trouble is, I can't really see what I am doing!" Of course she can't, bless her heart, as she has her back to the light. She must turn around to the window and face the light.

That is the trouble with some people who say they cannot "see" the gospel. They are standing in their own light. They think too much of themselves. All the light is in Jesus Christ, but people are in darkness because they put themselves in the way of His light. If only they would move to one side, stand in the light, and behold the Lamb of God who has borne away the sin of the world—and their sin—they would be healed.

A word of caution: when you are healed, get out of the company of diseased people. Remember that, for disease is infectious. Break with companionships which have infected you with sin; stand clear and confess the name of Jesus. Confess Him in personal testimony at your work. Dedicate your life to the great task of winning others for Him. When you are healed, stand clear for the Lord, for it is by His stripes that you are healed.

Precious, precious blood of Jesus,
    Shed on Calvary;
Shed for rebels, shed for sinners,
    Shed for thee.

FRANCES RIDLEY HAVERGAL

9

Isaiah 53:6-9

God's Remedy for Sin

All we like sheep have gone astray; we have turned every one to his own way; and the Lord hath laid on him the iniquity of us all.

Isaiah 53:6

As we now consider the great subject of God's remedy for sin, first note the nature of sin as it is described in the text verse, which contains the very heart of the gospel message. The human race is pictured as a flock of lost sheep, wandering about in stupidity and stubbornness. Like sheep, we read, not like an ox which knows its owner, not like an ass which remembers its master's crib, but like a sheep—a creature which is cared for by the shepherd and is incapable of gratitude towards the hand that cares for it. It is a creature with enough initiative to find a hole in the fence somewhere, force its way through, and become lost, but with neither the ability nor the desire to turn back and find the place from which it has wandered. Habitually, constantly, willfully, foolishly, men too have gone astray, says Isaiah, and are powerless to return on their own to the Lord.

I would interject a word at this point: this is a very different picture from the one given to us these days in modern thinking. Today men stand on a mountain peak. They look back over long periods of success and achievement, and look forward with tremendous hope, believing that the whole human race is really walking into a wonderful new day. Sin is nothing to worry about; it is merely a relic of the animal from which we have

85

evolved, and as evolution continues its process, it will be eliminated altogether. Yet, in spite of this very light statement and outlook upon the question, no one would deny that pacts and treaties by the thousand have brought this poor world no nearer the desire of its heart, no nearer to the righting of wrongs, no nearer to the healing of its wounds.

Surely there is no one who can really face present situations in the world today without recognizing there is something tragically wrong with human nature. The same evil that attacks us now has always attacked mankind, right throughout human history. This world has never been free of war or cruelty, because these things are the outcome of something wrong deep down in the human heart. Every child born into the world carries the infection, and therefore every generation starts again with exactly the same problem.

We do not touch the root of the trouble, however, if we imagine that sin is no more than a disease from which we are the unfortunate sufferers. In our last study we looked upon the disease aspect of sin, noting that it was incurable, but also that God had done something about it on our behalf. But now we see another side of the problem of sin: "All we like sheep have gone astray. . . ." But notice the next phrase: "We have turned every one to his own way." In other words, sin carries personal responsibility and guilt. The world is what it is because we are what we are, and the evil from which the whole world suffers has its roots in every one of our hearts. You see, in our own little world we behave very much as the rulers do in the big world, if I may put it like that. If they are proud, so are we. If they are unreasonable, so are we. If they are bitter, hard, unloving, so are we. If they are unforgiving, all out for selfish ends and personal interests, so are we. The Apostle James puts it like this: "From whence come wars and fightings among you? come they not hence, even of your lusts that war in your members?" (James 4:1). The Word of God, therefore, makes it perfectly clear that until our hearts are cleansed and our nature is renewed, we need never expect that the world will be free from strife and bitterness, corruption and sin.

It is very easy, from just a simple statement like that concerning world conditions, to see a little bit of the potency and power of sin in the human heart, but I cannot truly understand what sin is until I see Calvary. If I would know the measure of sin, I can only do so in the light of the cross of Jesus Christ.

Supposing a visitor from another planet alighted on this earth and asked us, "What sort of a world is this?" I think the truest and most relevant reply would be that this is the world which crucified the Son of God when He came to visit it. Such is our sin that we have found the presence of holiness intolerable. Such is the failure, the breakdown, the sinfulness of the human heart that incarnate goodness and love has to be put away.

I do not want to elaborate on this, but that is why so many people stop coming to church. It is not because there is anything inherently good in the church, not because there is holiness as there ought to be, but simply that there the message of God's requirements for our lives is presented to them, and an unbeliever cannot stand in the presence of that demand. Yes, the only adequate measure of sin is Calvary. ". . . this is the condemnation, that light is come into the world, and men loved darkness rather than light, because their deeds were evil" (John 3:19).

May the Spirit of God allow that truth to sink into our minds so that we might begin to see the hopelessness of our plight. I say this not to the unbelieving heart only, but to many a Christian who has rejected the light of God somewhere along the journey, who has turned against the cross as it reveals and unmasks the horror of sin in the heart. I am speaking to you just as much as to the unbeliever, as one who has been faced somewhere with the implications of God's demand for holiness, and the principle of the cross has been rejected. Now this is the nature of sin, that light has come, but because of selfish and evil living, men prefer darkness to light.

In the second place, we see here God's provision for sin. And just what is it? "The Lord hath laid on him the iniquity of us all." This is the great central truth of the gospel, that the Lord Jesus was not merely a great Teacher, but He was the Lamb of God slain from before the foundation of the world, who bears away the sin of the world—your sin and my sin—in His body on the tree.

And on His thorn-crowned head,
    And on His sinless soul,
Our sins in all their guilt were laid,
    That He might make us whole.

Countless multitudes of people have received that truth as
the very charter of their salvation. They believe that Christ by
His death has made atonement for the sin of the world, and they
have applied this by faith to their own personal lives, thereby
finding peace with God and deliverance from the guilt of sin.
I want you to think about this, because admittedly there is a
mystery here, something that baffles explanation.

What did the cross mean to Jesus?

What did the cross do for the heart of God?

What did it accomplish in heaven?

Of course, in one sense, this is something beyond our understanding. If it were not too vast for our minds to understand, it
would be far too small for our spiritual rest and enjoyment. But
this much we can say about the sufferings of our Lord upon
Calvary: they were voluntary and were unimposed upon Jesus
by some harsh decree. "I lay down my life," He said, ". . . No
man taketh it from me, but I lay it down of myself. I have power
to lay it down, and I have power to take it again" (John 10:-
17,18).

It is not a question of an angry God bent on vengeance, whose
wrath can only be appeased at great cost. That is a travesty of
the atonement. It is God who, because of His holiness, has pro-
nounced the sentence of judgment upon sin, and it is God who
has allowed that sentence to fall upon Himself. It was voluntary
on the part of His beloved Son.

Not only so, but His sacrifice was vicarious: "The Lord has
made to meet upon Him the iniquity of us all." That which was
scattered everywhere is brought into a dreadful concentration
upon the Lord Jesus, and all the sin of His people is caused to
meet upon Him.

I have a faint illustration of this, because no human illustration can in any way fully reveal this truth. Outside my study at
Moody Church, Chicago, was a flat roof on which I would occasionally walk. Though it did not exactly have a country view, I
found it somewhat relaxing, and an opportunity for quiet and

meditation. On one afternoon at about three o'clock I was out there. It became very dark, and there was a strange stillness about, and as I looked up inky clouds seemed to be moving in all directions, from north to south and from east to west. They were all converging together on one point almost above me, and it became darker and darker, almost like midnight. Street and window lights were switched on. I always thought the wind blew in one direction, but not here apparently! The clouds were gathering from every point, all coming to one focal spot, when suddenly, as I looked, there was a vivid stroke of lightning, a tremendous clap of thunder, and almost immediately a downpour of rain. The storm had broken. Everything had concentrated upon one spot, and then it all broke.

The Lord has caused to meet upon Him, the Lord Jesus, from every direction—north, south, east, west—the sins of the past, the present, and the future, like a tornado, the sins of us all. It was put on His back like a burden. It was placed upon His head as the High Priest laid upon the scapegoat all the sin of the people. God has caused to meet upon Him the sin of us all.

I would remind you that none but Jesus would be capable of a transaction like that. In His divine nature He is "holy, the Lord of Hosts." In His human nature, in view of His virgin birth, He is free from all original sin. By virtue of His holy life He is the Lamb of God without spot and without blemish. So on all counts He is the only One who is capable of standing in the place of guilty men before a holy God.

Oh, let us marvel at that in our hearts! He is the holy One from before the foundation of the world. Conceived by the Holy Spirit, born of a virgin; taking all the corruption of the human heart, yet living a spotless, pure, holy life. That, all together, makes Him God's perfect Lamb, the one and only Saviour, who alone is capable of having placed upon Him the sin of the world. Hallelujah, what a Saviour!

Someone may ask, "I don't understand why God should demand a sacrifice at all. Why can He not just forgive us? Surely He has power to do that!"

This suggests a shallow view of the atonement and of what sin really is, for Christ's suffering was not only voluntary and vicarious, but it was victorious.

I recognize that this is something far beyond our own human

understanding, but let me suggest to you that the judgment of
God upon sin is not primarily the punishment of sin, but the
establishment of His absolute holiness. You see, there was a
cloud between God and men which made salvation impossible
until His holiness was acknowledged and confessed in the judgment of sin. I can only be justified by faith in God who first of
all has justified Himself; and He has justified Himself by being
utterly holy, and He has set up holiness at any price, even that
of His well-beloved Son. True, the cross passes judgment upon
the foulest sin. But the cross does much more than that; it
establishes the eternal righteousness of God.

Once I was taken by a minister friend into Forest Lawn
Cemetery in California, and saw that amazing picture of the
Crucifixion conceived, I believe, by the pianist Jan Paderewski.
There it faces you, twenty stories high if it was up on end. As
you watch and listen to the tape recording explaining the picture, your heart is gripped, as mine was, by one thing. That
picture, as you may know, does not show Christ on the cross. It
shows Him standing at the moment before the actual crucifixion took place. Around Him are the priests and soldiers, the
women, Mary His mother, and Peter; in the distance are
Nicodemus and Joseph of Arimathea; and in the background,
the city wall. Behind Him are the two thieves ready to be nailed
to their crosses. There is the cross of Jesus flat upon the ground,
and standing beside it is the Lord. Somehow the artist has captured the look of victory, of quiet, calm majesty, of purity and
holiness, that seems to shame everything around. When I saw
that picture I caught in my heart again the thrill of the victorious cross: not simply punishing sin (though it is true He was
made sin for us), but more than that, for as Jesus hung upon the
cross He was confessing to God His absolute holiness, His absolute authority and total power, and He was establishing eternal
righteousness. He was not just letting people who had gone into
sin into heaven by some kind of cheap way, ushering them in
the back door, saying, "It's going to be all right!" No, but by
establishing absolute righteousness, and making it possible for
all men to come to Him on that basis. This is the cross, God's
perfect and only provision.

Ah, but something more important than either of these

things, in the third place, is the cleansing of sin. We have been thinking about two objective facts: first, the nature of sin, and secondly, God's provision and remedy for sin. But how does this affect you and me? How do these two objective facts fit together, and how do I find my place in them?

Before I take a third and last brief look at our text, let me ask you a question. Do you think Christianity is merely human nature at its best, brought under the influence of religion and self-sacrifice? Everything else in the world apart from the church is built upon the lines of what is called brotherhood, humanity, goodness, and so on, but not the church or the Christian gospel. That is a total contradiction of divine revelation. You see, the Christian faith is not human nature deified, but it is God Himself coming down to deliver man. It is not we who attain to our most wonderful state because of the example of self-sacrifice of the Lord Jesus at Calvary. It is God in Christ delivering us from ourselves.

Let me show you this by illustration. Conjure up in your mind some great deed of heroism. There are many recorded almost every week in the press, and we all thrill with a sense of wonder to someone who may have risked his life to rescue another. He became a victim in order that he might save the life of another. But is that the true meaning of the cross? No. Suppose you add together every deed of heroism that has ever been committed in all history, would that all add up to Calvary? No. Everyone thrills to the story of a hero. Nobody thrills to the message of Calvary.

There is something within human nature which leaps to respond to an act of heroism and thinks it wonderful, and so it is. But there is nothing within us that is capable of responding to Christ upon the cross. How true that it was "when we were yet without strength, in due time Christ died for the ungodly" (Romans 5:6). It was when we were without power or feeling, when we were utterly dead that Christ died on our behalf. We are not asked to respond to heroism, but to God's deliverance from ourselves, the judgment of sin in our lives, and to His holiness.

Every preacher knows how easy it is to produce tears. Stories about children who have died in agony, some terrible escapes from fire, produce an emotional response involving tears. Then, of course, on that basis one could make an evangelistic appeal and fill the aisles with people—but that would be doing the work of the devil. The cross does not call for our admiration or enthusiasm. It does not demand that we put up a replica and follow after Jesus as a great adventure. It calls for us to be on our faces in repentance, for a confession of our shame, our guilt, and the acknowledgment of utter, complete sinfulness.

The cross of Jesus Christ has to turn the man who is an enemy into a friend. It does not touch some spark of life with us, as heroism does. It does not kindle some dormant spark of friendship for God. No, no—the acceptance of the full meaning of Calvary starts a totally new creation in our lives by His Spirit, when for the first time we experience the love of God shed abroad in our hearts by the Holy Ghost which is given to us (*see* Romans 5:5). The cross is not to do with our dullness but with our hostility. Therefore, wherever the message of redemption through Christ is preached and clearly sounded out it creates antagonism, because men want to cling to the last rags of their self-respect. How much of that do you think the Apostle Paul had when he met the risen Lord Jesus on the road to Damascus? He had none, for all his pride was stripped from him completely.

A hero is welcomed by the crowds, but only the few welcome Jesus. For when He comes to grips with a man's heart he has to come down from his pedestal. He has to be literally pulverized that the living Lord might create in him a new nature from the wreck of his egotism and pride. That is the cross. It brings to an end all self-confidence, and it starts a new principle of life altogether.

Puritan preachers used to say that the congregation needed to be shaken over the pit. Maybe we do today, to realize that the Lord has plucked us from a fearful pit and from the miry clay, and set our feet upon the Rock.

In the light of that, take a last look at our text, Isaiah 53:6. With a hatred of God, a hatred of truth, and a hatred of spiritual things which has been brought about by His absolute.holiness, we have turned every one to our own way. Crowds will respond to a sentimental approach to the cross, but when I understand there is a revelation of God's judgment of sin, a confession of His absolute holiness, then I see the cross is either a savor of life or of death, and that is the whole implication of our text.

Listen to it again: "All we like sheep have gone astray [that is general confession]; we have turned every one to his own way [that is personal repentance]." It is always a mark of genuine repentance of heart when it gets a man out of the crowd and in the loneliness of his own soul he cries out, "God, be merciful to ME, a sinner!" That is the essence of repentance. It takes up a place of utter aloneness before God. Each one of us has sinned in a way that no one else has, peculiar to ourselves, unknown to other people; and you will observe from the text there is no syllable of excuse, not a word of self-justification. Merely to say "we have sinned" means nothing, but to acknowledge, *"I* have sinned, and *I* am guilty" causes us to stand with our weapons of rebellion taken from us and shattered in pieces. That is what the cross does for us. That is the first step that makes us ready for the remedy of God for the sin of our lives.

Has your repentance been personal? Have you stood in the loneliness of your heart in the presence of God and said, "Lord, against Thee and Thee only have I sinned"? It doesn't mean much to say when you come to church, "Forgive us our sins," and really it does not mean much to say that on your own in prayer. Ah, but in the secrecy of your soul before God to say, "Lord, *I* have sinned" is to find that at that moment, and in that place, God's remedy is applied to your heart and life.

The second step that leads a man to the application of the remedy is not merely the step of personal aloneness in repentance, but it is a personal step of faith. Listen to the language of Romans 8:33,34: "Who shall lay any thing to the charge of God's elect? It is God that justifieth. Who is he that condemneth? It is Christ that died, yea rather, that is risen again, who is even at the right hand of God, who also maketh intercession for us."

Here then are the two requirements for the application of the remedy: a personal lonely repentance, a personal living faith.

This message has tremendous relevance to Christians today. How many have turned their back upon the light in some area of their life, and have followed a course which has cut them off from fellowship with God! I quote a very solemn verse: "For if we sin wilfully after that we have received the knowledge of the truth, there remaineth no more sacrifice for sins, But a certain fearful looking for of judgment and fiery indignation, which shall devour the adversaries. He that despised Moses' law died without mercy under two or three witnesses: Of how much sorer punishment, suppose ye, shall he be thought worthy, who hath trodden under foot the Son of God, and hath counted the blood of the covenant, wherewith he was sanctified, an unholy thing, and hath done despite unto the Spirit of grace?" (Hebrews 10:26-29).

If I speak to one who has been a professing Christian, yet you have shut your ears to the Word and your eyes to the light, turning your back upon the truth and following a course today that you know is wrong (though you try to make Scripture prove it not to be so), then I would warn you of these solemn words in the Epistle to the Hebrews. You need aloneness with God for repentance. This is the way back into fellowship. You need a living faith, that when you confess your sin alone to Him, He is gracious and willing to forgive.

> O Lamb of God, Thou wonderful Sin-bearer,
>   Hard after Thee my soul doth follow on;
> As pants the hart for streams in desert dreary,
> So pants my soul for Thee, O Thou life-giving One.
>
> I mourn, I mourn the sin that drove Thee from me,
>   And blackest darkness brought into my soul;
> Now I renounce the cursed thing that hindered,
> And come once more to Thee, to be made fully whole.
>
> Come, Holy Ghost, Thy mighty aid bestowing,
>   Destroy the work of sin, the self, the pride;
> Burn, burn in me, my idols overthrowing,
> Prepare my heart for Him—for my Lord crucified!
>
>   At Thy feet I fall, yield Thee up my all,
>   To suffer, live, or die, for my Lord crucified.

MRS. BOOTH-CLIBBORN

10

Isaiah 53:7

When Silence is Golden

He was oppressed, and he was afflicted, yet he opened not his mouth: he is brought as a lamb to the slaughter, and as a sheep before her shearers is dumb, so he openeth not his mouth.

Isaiah 53:7

We have been considering in some detail the message of this chapter and the price that was paid by the Lord Jesus on our behalf at Calvary. Now we turn our attention to the attitude of the Saviour in the face of suffering. This verse might be rendered: He was hard pressed and humbled Himself, yet He opened not His mouth.

Those last few words are repeated again, suggesting that the preeminent aspect of His attitude to His sufferings was silence. It was said of the Lord Jesus that never man spoke like He did, but it is also true that never man was silent as He was.

Let us recall, by way of introduction, the last moments of our Lord's life here on earth.

(1) Before Caiaphas (Matthew 26:62-64). Here He stood before the High Priest, accused of blasphemy. He was silent, except when to remain silent would have been to deny His claim to deity.

(2) Before Pilate (Matthew 27:11-14). It is recorded here how He stood before the Roman governor, accused of treason. He was silent, except when to remain so would have been to deny His claim to kingship.

(3) Before the whole band of soldiers (Matthew 27:28-30).

They stripped Him, crowned Him with thorns, blindfolded Him, spat on Him, smote Him with a reed, struck Him in the face, and mocked Him. Not a single word crossed His lips. At one word from Him in the Garden of Gethsemane, in one brief flashing glimpse of His power, they all fell to the ground. Here He restrained His omnipotence. One glance to heaven and a volcano could have opened in the ground and swallowed up all who opposed Him. What a tremendous display of power was the silence which restrained Him in the face of the scorn of His enemies!

(4) Before Herod (Luke 23:8,9). Christ was questioned regarding many things, yet He answered not a word to the man who had sinned away his opportunity and forfeited every claim upon the salvation of God. Faced by John the Baptist with his immoral life, Herod refused to give up the woman who ruined him. It is a terrifying possibility to sit under a ministry, to sense conviction, yet to refuse to forsake sin! To such a man Jesus was silent.

(5) At Calvary (Matthew 27:45,46). There was darkness for three hours, and silence. Hell did its worst, let loose all its fury, yet He was silent, broken only at the ninth hour by that awesome cry, "My God, my God, why hast thou forsaken me?"

Yes, the preeminent thing about His suffering was His silence. Before all His accusers and tormentors He spoke not one word of complaint, only of testimony. Not once did He seek to plead His innocence, only to claim His authority. Truly, He was hard pressed and humbled Himself, yet He opened not His mouth. He is brought as a lamb to the slaughter, and as a sheep before her shearers is dumb, so He opened not His mouth.

We can only bow in wonder and worship. Why the silence? The answer of the world is in Isaiah 53:4, ". . . we did esteem him stricken, smitten of God, and afflicted." That is, He must be guilty of all they charged Him with, otherwise a loving God would not have allowed it to happen. But we cannot accept such an explanation, for the whole revelation of Scripture contradicts it.

What, then, does this silence mean? In seeking to answer that question we do so not merely to understand His silence in its bearing upon His life and testimony, but also to recognize its message for our own hearts. The cross has a twofold implication: it spells redemption from sin, but also—and as a sequel to that redemption—identification with the One who suffered at Calvary in displaying the whole principle of Christian living to others (*see* Galatians 2:20).

In some aspects the Lord Jesus is unique, yet I can learn from His silence the times when silence is golden in my own experience, also.

Let us consider *the silence of decisiveness in commitment to the will of God*. Compare two very important Scriptures. In Acts 2:23, He was "delivered by the determinate counsel and foreknowledge of God." In John 4:34, "Jesus saith unto them, My meat is to do the will of him that sent me, and to finish his work."

Does not His silence declare His refusal to utter one word to prevent His death, since He was committed to the will of God to be a sacrifice for us? So entirely and decisively was He surrendered that He would not interfere on His own behalf, even in the slightest degree, but rather be bound and slain without struggle and without complaint. There was no reservation; body, soul, and spirit were wholly given up to the Father's will. Not one faculty He possessed asked to be excused. Every limb of His body, every thought of His mind, every desire of His spirit, was in submission. It was a whole Christ giving up His whole being to God, that He might offer Himself without reservation and without spot for our redemption.

Would that your commitment and mine to His will was as decisive as that! To resign ourselves completely, to deliver up our entire life in self-conquest to God! To find ourselves absorbed in one desire for His will! To see the sacrifice accepted, as was Elijah's on Mount Carmel, and to have the answering fire from heaven "burn up the dross of base desire, and make the mountains flow"! When the fire consumed not only the bullock and the wood, but also licked up the water in the trench, the whole of Elijah's sacrifice ascended to heaven in a cloud of fire and smoke, and was a complete burnt offering to the living God. Oh, that He would do that for us today, and settle forever our arguments and disputes concerning our right to ourselves! What right have we, in the light of the Lord Jesus refusing His own? As the priest in Old Testament times used the fleshhook to keep the sacrifice under the flame, surely the Lord has to do that to us. Perhaps even at this moment you could make the wonderful words of George Matheson your prayer:

> Make me a captive, Lord,
>   And then I shall be free;
> Force me to render up my sword,
>   And I shall conqueror be.
> I sink in life's alarms
>   When by myself I stand;
> Imprison me within Thine arms,
>   And strong shall be my hand.
>
> My will is not my own
>   Till Thou hast made it Thine;
> If it would reach the monarch's throne
>   It must its crown resign;
> It only stands unbent
>   Amid the clashing strife,
> When on Thy bosom it has leant,
>   And found in Thee its life.

Consider now *the silence of disdainfulness in contempt for the enemies of God.* Jesus Christ did not accuse them of injustice. He did not reply to slander, nor did He answer false witnesses. To argue with those who were bent on His murder would have been futile, and the result would only have been greater fury and further sin. Rather, as the Apostle Peter reminds us, "... when he was reviled, [he] reviled not again; when he suffered, he threatened not; but committed himself to him that judgeth righteously" (1 Peter 2:23).

The best reply to false accusation is silence, yet how quick we are to rise up in self-defense! How sensitive we are to criticism, and how eager we are to prove ourselves right!

When David was harassed by Saul, his life-long enemy, on at least two occasions he had a wonderful opportunity finally to deal with him and kill him, but he refused. Even when his right-hand man, Abishai, offered to do it for him, David refused to allow him to do so, saying, "As the Lord liveth, the Lord shall smite him; or his day shall come to die; or he shall descend into battle, and perish. The Lord forbid that I should stretch forth mine hand against the Lord's anointed" (1 Samuel 26:10,11). David exercised marvelous restraint, and by his attitude is a slight reflection of his greater Son who did not answer back when insulted, when He suffered He did not threaten to get even, but rather left His case in the hands of His Father who always judges righteously and justly.

Has the Lord taught you that lesson? It is a costly one, and the flesh revolts against it, crying out for recognition and vindication. It shrinks from being put in a bad light in the eyes of others, but what a blessed release when the Christian learns to commit himself to Him that judges righteously, and allows Him to deal with the situation. This does not necessarily mean that in this life he is proved right, but it does mean the assent of the flesh to the principle of death, and therefore the anointing of the life with the power of the Holy Spirit, and that is all that matters. How many a Christian has lost that anointing for the sake of trying to defend himself, and how ready we all are to judge other people without knowing all the facts. May the Lord teach us all when silence is golden!

Dr. Roland Bingham tells the story of a rising young executive who, at Christmas, was given a turkey, as were all others in similar positions in his office. This young man was a bachelor, and the girls were always fluttering around him. On this occasion he went out to lunch, leaving the turkey wrapped up on his desk. While he was away the girls came in a giggling flurry into his office, unwrapped the turkey, and cut off all the flesh from the bones, filling the carcass with paper clips, staples, wastepaper, and anything they could lay their hands on to make the package the original weight. Their handiwork completed, they wrapped the bird up again, and left it on the young man's desk.

Later in the day as he returned to his bachelor apartment by bus, an older, sad-looking man came and sat beside him.

"That's a big parcel you have," he remarked, looking at the package on the young man's lap. "Looks like a turkey."

"Yes, it is, and actually I will not be using it as I always eat out at Christmas."

"You are fortunate. I have seven children, no work, and I'm trying to get something for Christmas with the small amount of money I have."

"How much do you have?" asked the young man.

"I have two dollars."

"All right; give me your two dollars and you can have the turkey."

The exchange was made to the satisfaction of both parties.

When the young man got to his office after the holidays, the girls came in, giggling, asking how he enjoyed his Christmas, and if the turkey was a good one. He told them the story of the poor man on the bus, and at once there was an intense silence, until one of the girls confessed what they had done to the turkey. The whole office staff was thoroughly convicted of its ill-conceived jocularity, and the first thing the young man did was to try to find the man, which he utterly failed to do. Worse than this, the young executive was also a local preacher, and from that time on he refused to preach in the whole area for fear the man he had unwittingly wronged was in the congregation, waiting to point a finger at him and accuse him of what to him must have seemed a confidence trick of the meanest order.

Finally, look at *the silence of defenselessness in consent to the judgment of God*. There is a meaning of His silence deeper than anything yet considered in this study. Nothing can be said to excuse human guilt, therefore He who bore its full weight stood speechless before the judge. "He was led as a sheep to the slaughter."

Do you see how completely He is identified with us? "All we like sheep . . ." (v. 6). Not only are we compared with sheep, but so is He. I can understand that we could be likened to sheep and He to the Shepherd; but that He, too, should be likened to a sheep, who but God dare make that comparison? Yet it is the theme of Scripture: "Behold the Lamb of God" (John 1:29)—He became what we were in order that we might become what He is. "For he hath made him to be sin for us, who knew no sin; that we might be made the righteousness of God in him" (2 Corinthians 5:21).

Here then is the deepest meaning of His silence. The law had spoken: ". . . what things soever the law saith, it saith to them who are under the law: that every mouth may be stopped, and all the world may become guilty before God" (Romans 3:19). A condemned world with no argument to plead, no excuse to make, silently awaits the sentence of its doom. But, praise God, in place of a silent world stands a silent Saviour, led as a lamb to the slaughter and opening not His mouth before His accusers. There He stands in my place, defenseless, as He consents to bear the judgment due to me. The silence of Jesus!

That is a lonely road along which none of us can travel, for He trod it alone. Yet there *is* something I can do, and indeed I must do if I am to enter into the significance of this message to my heart, and the same applies to you.

Have you ever stood in the presence of the Lord with bowed head and heart, silent, with no excuses, no arguments, no complaints, and said, "Lord, I am wrong; You are right. I consent to judgment, but I am absolutely defenseless, and I am looking to my Saviour, the Lord Jesus, upon whose merits I rest."

Perhaps you have resented those who have spoken about you wrongly, and have thereby forfeited much of the anointing of the Spirit upon your life. Bring this in confession to the One who bore so much hatred silently. As you reflect in His presence the long, hard, lonely road to Calvary upon which the Saviour walked on your behalf, look again at your own commitment to His will and purpose for your life. "Lord, I am ashamed at my hesitating, halfhearted commitment, and come now to lay down the arms of my rebellion at Thy feet."

True humility is the silence of the soul before God, when there are no more debates or arguments. May He give us this wonderful grace.

11

Isaiah 53:10,11

How to Satisfy God

When thou shalt make his soul an offering for sin, he shall see his seed, he shall prolong his days, and the pleasure of the Lord shall prosper in his hand. He shall see of the travail of his soul, and shall be satisfied.

Isaiah 53:10,11

I shall never understand in fullness our text until I see the Lord face-to-face. How to bring it home to your heart in all its beauty and majesty and greatness is beyond me. May the Holy Spirit reveal the grace of God through His Word.

Have you ever stopped and turned your thoughts upon this word *satisfy*? It is rather an unusual word. "He shall see of the travail of his soul, and shall be *satisfied.*"

Are you satisfied? am I? I question it. True, we say that Jesus satisfies, but the vast majority of Christians indicate by the way they live that He does not, or else they would not be so taken up with material things. But does He satisfy? In some measure, yes; but would it not be true and honest to say that the average experience of most Christians is not satisfaction but frustration? I do not meet many who are really satisfied. Of course, there is a sense in which to say we are satisfied would be smug and pious and proud, but I do not mean that.

Consider prayerfully a cross and the crucified Lord Jesus; an empty tomb and the ascended Christ; the enthroned Saviour and outpoured Holy Spirit. Now if you are honest, as you think about all this, does it not bring a sense of shame at the poverty of your own experience? Yet I do believe that there is a way in which every one of us may enter into a satisfied life, not in any smug sense, but in a way which God would have us enjoy it.

You do not enter into a satisfied life by busy Christian work. That becomes extremely frustrating. You go round and round in circles until you become bone dry, putting up a performance that is of no value either to the cause of Christ or to anyone else. That is not satisfaction.

A Christian enters into a satisfied life when he enters into fellowship with his Lord. As he gets alone with God and close to His heart, he begins to say, "Master, *Thou* art satisfied, for I read 'Thou shalt see of the travail of Thy soul, and shall be satisfied.' Lord, I am Thy child and a member of Thy family: can I not be satisfied, too?" Of course you can, because the way in which God is satisfied is exactly the way in which His children are satisfied.

Let us look first at *the cause of the satisfaction of God* objectively, from the standpoint of heaven; then view it subjectively from the standpoint of the life of the believer.

As you read Isaiah 53, notice that God speaks about satisfaction in the midst of a poignant description of suffering: ". . . it pleased the Lord to bruise him; he hath put him to grief: when thou shalt make his soul an offering for sin, he shall see his seed, he shall prolong his days, and the pleasure of the Lord shall prosper in his hand. He shall see of the travail of his soul, and shall be satisfied."

In other words, God is satisfied in the midst of travail. Or to state the same truth in basic simplicity, there is never any satisfaction in a self-centered life. Speaking reverently, even God could never have known perfect blessedness and utter satisfaction unless He had been able to pour Himself out in blessing to others. Therefore, this reference to satisfaction is found with the context of the account of His travail. Whatever may have been the joy which our Lord Jesus had with the Father from before the foundation of the world, it was absolutely nothing compared with the eternal joy in His heart which followed the experience of the cross.

Now see this truth expressed in four simple sentences:

1. There is no satisfaction without love.
2. There is no love without travail.
3. There is no travail without joy.
4. The measure of the travail governs the depth of joy.

It is around these four sentences that the message of this study is entwined.

As these thoughts are considered in the light of Calvary, I am sure that the physical suffering of the Lord Jesus was almost imperceptible to Him compared with the pressure of those stripes by which we are healed. He was wounded not only in His flesh, but He was mortally wounded in His heart as He was bruised by the justice of God. He stood before the whole universe, charged with the sin of all the world, and He tasted death for every man. In the one act He put away sin, He exhausted its penalty, He wiped out its guilt, and He satisfied the justice of heaven. ". . . for the joy that was set before him [Jesus] endured the cross, despising the shame, and is set down at the right hand of the throne of God" (Hebrews 12:2).

The cause of God's satisfaction is the cross in His heart.

Consider now *the continuance of God's satisfaction.*

The cross is not simply an act of history but in one sense it is something that is being repeated every day. Of course, it was a finished work, but nevertheless listen to what our text says: ". . . when thou shalt make his soul an offering for sin, he shall see his seed. . . . He shall see of the travail of his soul, and shall be satisfied."

The sense of dissatisfaction in the heart of any reader is rooted in the fact of sin, which should drive you to the cross, the only place where you can look when your heart is so burdened that you are overwhelmed. When perhaps you have been conscious of some fall, or you are baffled by some problem or sin that brings guilt and shame, how blessed it is to approach the mercy seat and to find that already He has made His soul an offering for your sin! He sees of the travail of His soul, and is satisfied. The harvest of His tears and blood is reaped.

I know that the harvest of sin is dreadful, but I am absolutely sure that the harvest of salvation will be far greater, for surely those who are saved will vastly outnumber those who are lost.

When the Apostle John recorded in the Book of Revelation the firstfruits of salvation, he saw a multitude that no man could number, redeemed by the blood of the Lamb. I too, in my imagination, behold the myriads upon myriads of people throughout countless generations who have put their faith in the blood of the Lord Jesus. Some of them are perhaps little children who were too young to understand, yet are among those who have been caught up into heaven in the tenderest of years into the very presence of Christ. I think of the martyrs, and people of every tribe and nation, some perhaps never numbered in any earthly church, yet who constitute the great harvest of the cross, that which is the secret of the continued satisfaction in the heart of God. He gave His life a ransom for many—how many? Only God knows, but He shall be satisfied.

The cause of His satisfaction is the cross in His heart. The continuance of it is the constant confession of sin and the coming to Him of one after another, men and women who have found life absolutely futile and disastrous without Him.

Now think of *the completion of God's satisfaction.* "He shall see of the travail of his soul, and shall be satisfied." I like to think of that day yet to be when the Lord Jesus will present His bride, His church, to His Father in heaven without spot or wrinkle or any such thing, perfect, without fault or blame, before the throne of God, with exceeding joy. In every believer the mark of Satan will have been obliterated and replaced by the seal of the Lord Jesus, as His bride is presented in spotless purity to the Father.

Yes, men and women will be brought far nearer to God in redemption through the blood of His beloved Son than they could ever have been had they remained unfallen in the Garden of Eden. For God has made His tabernacle with His people and come to dwell with them in the person of His Son who with His life paid the price of their redemption. One day, when the "Hallelujah Chorus" breaks out in glory from myriads of souls who have been ransomed, *then* He shall see of the travail of His soul, and shall be satisfied.

When God put His hand to the task of redeeming men, He knew He would triumph. There was never any doubt about it at all. As we see Him emptying Himself of His glory, stooping down to Bethlehem and Calvary, then look in vain for Him in the tomb because He arose from the dead, we know that there is no question about it. The completion of God's satisfaction is a pure, holy, spotless church—the perfect bride for His beloved Son.

This subject has been considered briefly and objectively, so now look at it subjectively. Someone may say, "Do you mean to tell me that I can be satisfied like that?" The answer is *yes*. For every objective fact and truth about the cross there is a subjective truth in our experience. Of course, I recognize that the Lord Jesus trod the winepress alone, and no mere human can ever share in that great work of redemption, yet nevertheless there is a very real measure in which the way God's heart is satisfied is exactly the same way as the heart of an individual right now can be satisfied, too, and in no other way.

How would you explain that, you ask?

Well, what does the text say? Please put your name in as you read the verse: "When. . . . shalt make His soul an offering for . . . sin [what does He see?], He shall see His seed." In other words, at that moment, when you receive Christ into your heart and crown Him Lord of your life, God implants into your personality the seed of eternal life.

Sometimes we are inclined to think of eternal life as a gift that God gives us, but this is not true. Many people believe the phrase refers purely to duration, that life lasts forever, but this is not true either. Everyone lives forever, and the acceptance of Christ does not affect that. But it does affect your destiny. If death was annihilation, if the coffin was the end, then how meaningless is all existence. But death is not the end, and every life goes on for an endless eternity, either in a hell of judgment or in a heaven of grace and salvation. God gives to us eternal life, and that means He gives us Himself. Yes, *HE* comes into the life of those who trust in Jesus. *HE* enters into the repentant, contrite, broken heart, into the life that is bankrupt because of sin. He implants the seed of His character, and that is eternal life. As He does so, He looks down to see the travail of His soul in that life, and to be satisfied, and He watches for the growth of that new life, which is His own life. He watches for

it to triumph; He guards and fosters it until one day that redeemed person stands without fault in His very presence. That
is eternal life.

What is the cause of the Christian's satisfaction? It is the cross
in his heart, the sharing of the travail, the pain, the agony, the
concern, the burden, in the heart of a holy, loving God for souls
who are lost. That is the seed that He plants, and some of you
have not spent five minutes praying for others who are without
Christ! You have been busy with your program, with a hundred
and one other things. A Christian without love or a burden for
men is a complete paradox, and such a person is not to be found
in Scripture.

Has heavenly love gripped your heart? Is there any travail
there? Are you saying daily, "My Jesus, I love Thee"? He looks
down into your heart and says, "There is no true love for Me
which does not go out to those I love." You cannot love a person
into the life of Christ without travail. One of the things that
shames my heart so often is that somehow through the years I
seem to have lost my ability to weep for those who do not know
my Saviour. Yet the principle of harvest is as real today as it ever
has been: "He that goeth forth and weepeth, bearing precious
seed, shall doubtless come again with rejoicing, bringing his
sheaves with him" (Psalm 126:6).

There is no satisfaction without love; no love without travail;
no travail without joy, and no joy without blessedness. The
measure of travail is the measure of joy.

Bring to mind those who serve the Lord in some lonely mission station. I know they have wept. They have been so much
alone, and sometimes their tears may seem to have been in vain
because there has been little response. But I believe as tears are
shed drop by drop under the burden for a soul without Christ,
so the tide has turned, and the power of Satan broken. Nothing
else can do that.

At evangelistic crusades, crowds of inquirers come forward.
A considerable portion of them are there and then clearly,
completely, and happily converted, I am sure; but I would say
that the majority of them are confused and uncertain. Perhaps
that is the first impact they have ever had with the gospel; the
message has gone forth and their hearts have responded to the

truth, for they are seeking after something. Now how does that inquirer become a convert and a member of the church of Jesus Christ? Only by the tears of God's people and the travail of a united church. But so many Christians never attend prayer meetings, and because of this evangelism is shallow. Converts are not to be found in the church when evangelistic meetings are over, and do you know why? Because the church membership has never agonized over them. It is very easy to blame the evangelist, but the blame rests to a large extent upon the lack of love and burden of so many believers who reveal their lack of care by their lack of prayer.

If the tragedy of liberal churches is the high percentage of unconverted people in them, I suggest that the tragedy of the fundamental churches is the high percentage of Christians who do not reproduce. There is a sad breakdown of New Testament propagation of growth within the church.

How then can I, can you, satisfy God? What is the cause of His own satisfaction? It is by bearing the burden of the cross in our hearts, and by living as men and women with a consuming love and care for those who are still without the knowledge of the saving power of Christ.

Here, for example, is Mr. X. He is a regular attender at church, perhaps a church officer or a Sunday-school teacher, or he works among the young people, or maybe sings in the choir. He will occasionally be at a prayer meeting, and he maintains he is witnessing somewhere, in his business or perhaps by opening his house for a home-study group—but he never reproduces life. Someone has said that the success of any movement is in direct proportion to its ability to mobilize its entire membership to propagate its belief. That is why such cults as the Jehovah's Witnesses and Mormons get a grip on people. That is why Marxism floods the world. That is why Christianity in many areas is on the retreat.

The cross is the only real incentive for service. The question is not "what is God's program for missions?" God's program *is* missions. A church that ceases to have a missionary vision dies, and what is true of a church is, of course, true of the individual Christian. A child of God without a missionary vision is a contradiction in New Testament teaching, and such a person would probably find himself without a personal knowledge of the saving grace of the Lord Jesus.

What is the source of continued satisfaction in the Christian's life? Well, what was its source with God? It was the constant coming to Him, one by one, of those who availed themselves of the bloodstained mercy seat. What is the constant satisfaction in the heart of the believer? Surely it is the daily confession of the sinfulness of his own heart and calling sin *sin* in the presence of God.

"But," you may argue, "I am not conscious of any sin."

Are you sure? Have you stopped to examine your own heart about this?

"Oh," you say, "but when I came to Jesus I put the burden of all my sin on Him."

What have you been doing with the sin of the past seven days? Has not your daily walk with God made you increasingly sensitive? Are you excusing it or rationalizing it, calling it a mental or temperamental problem? What have you been doing with it?

Or have you come to Him today and every day with a constant, continued confession? For though you may have been a Christian for thirty years or more, you are no better than when you began. For "If we confess our sins, he is faithful and just to forgive us our sins, and to cleanse us from all unrighteousness" (1 John 1:9).

What is the completion of the Christian's satisfaction? What was the completion of it in the heart of God? The presenting before Himself of a bride without spot or stain. What, then, is the completion of our satisfaction as Christ's followers? The Psalmist has an answer to that question: "I shall be satisfied, when I awake, with thy likeness" (Psalm 17:15). It is as we seek day-by-day to be more like Him until one day we are received in His presence to receive the crown of righteousness that He places upon the character of a godly life. This was Paul's great goal as he wrote in Philippians 3:13,14, ". . . this one thing I do, forgetting those things which are behind, and reaching forth unto those things which are before, I press toward the mark for the prize of the high calling of God in Christ Jesus."

Lord crucified, give me a heart like Thine;
Teach me to love the dying souls of men,
And give me love, pure Calvary love,
To bring the lost to Thee.

12

Isaiah 54:1-10

The Key to a Fruitful Life

In a little wrath I hid my face from thee for a moment; but with everlasting kindness will I have mercy on thee, saith the Lord thy Redeemer.

Isaiah 54:8

It would seem that God would speak to us from these verses on what I have called *the discipline of the government of God.* As we recall the sequence of teaching in this section of Isaiah's prophecy, we read of God's call to His people concerning their release from captivity in Isaiah 52:11, "Depart ye, depart ye, go ye out from thence, touch no unclean thing." Then we read in Isaiah 53 of the Servant of Jehovah who became the sin bearer of His people and our sin bearer, too, at such infinite cost. Now in chapter 54 once again the desolation of Jerusalem is brought to the forefront. Notice how the Holy Spirit describes it. Remember that He is God, and therefore He cannot err: "O barren . . . the children of the desolate" (v. 1); ". . . the Lord hath called thee as a woman forsaken. . . . For a small moment have I forsaken thee" (vs. 6,7).

God is referring to His people as barren, desolate, forsaken—and the One who spoke those words cannot possibly be wrong. Indeed, they are underlined by the contemporary preacher of the time, Nehemiah: "Ye see the distress that we are in, how Jerusalem lieth waste, and the gates thereof are burned with fire" (Nehemiah 2:17). But how is this?

The Lord has put away sin at the cost of His wounds, His

111

stripes, His death. How then can Jerusalem lie as a sort of open sore upon the face of the earth? How can this continue to be? Cannot God's forgiveness, which has triumphed over sin, triumph also over the wreckage and damage which sin has caused? How can any redemption be complete if it fails to grapple with the fruit of our wrongdoing?

These questions open up a tremendous subject; it is one that touches every one of us, and from which none is excluded. May I lovingly probe into your heart? We are conscious that though sin, when it is repented of and forsaken, is forgiven, yet the consequences of it remain. The consequences of sin are seen here in the picture of a ruined city. The past cannot be undone —God Himself cannot undo the past. Those seventy years of captivity, with all the shame and sorrow involved, with all the lost opportunities, cannot just be wiped off as though they had never happened. It could never again be with Israel as though those years had never been, for they had left their mark.

Look back upon your Christian life. Pause and reflect upon periods of carelessness and prayerlessness; of sin, the memory of which is vivid and humiliating, resulting in a cold heart and perhaps a silent testimony. None of this affects the individual only: it is a family matter, and the family of God's people is affected.

Look at verse 5, where Isaiah uses the word *Redeemer,* and again in verse 8: ". . . with everlasting kindness will I have mercy on thee, saith the Lord thy Redeemer." The significance of the work of the Lord our Redeemer is brought out by comparing two verses of Scripture.

"Instead of the thorn shall come up the fir tree, and instead of the brier shall come up the myrtle tree" (Isaiah 55:13).

". . . as sin hath reigned unto death, even so might grace reign through righteousness unto eternal life by Jesus Christ our Lord" (Romans 5:21).

Do you not feel yourselves asking these questions sometimes, and wondering, "Must the life of a redeemed soul be fruitless?" "Must a man, having made his bed, lie on it?" "Though sin may be forgiven eternally, has it to haunt a man for the rest of his life?" "How does God deal with sin?"

Let me answer that by illustration.

Suppose a man is taken into custody because he is drunk and disorderly. There are two results which follow: in the first place he has broken the law of the country, and for this he is either fined or put in prison. In the second place, he has a headache, depression, and a nervous reaction, and these last three things follow that man long after his relationship to the law of the country has been put right, especially if he continues in the habit.

Or again (perhaps this is nearer home for some of us), a man is devoted to his business, so much so that he never has any time for his home or family, and night after night he is away from his children until they come to think of him as a complete stranger. They have no companionship with their father, and ultimately they have no confidence in him. The sacred ties of parenthood have been torn apart. The mother cannot supply the strength and firmness that is needed to hold the situation together, and almost without noticing it, imperceptibly through the years the family begins to drift apart. Years go by, and then the father wakes up with a shock when it is too late. Something has happened to one of his precious children. They are men and women now. They sought companionship and friendship away from their family, home, and parents, and this has led to disaster. Too late the father sees his mistake and tries to remedy it. The love of the children has gone beyond recall. He is forgiven by God, he is forgiven by his wife who has clung to him through the years, but he can never undo the damage of the past. For the rest of that man's life he stands amid the ruins of his Jerusalem.

There is no need to go outside the Bible to illustrate this. Put into the context of Scripture, when I sin against God two things happen. My sin cries out to heaven and its voice goes up to the throne, and it can only be silenced when in humility, repentance, and shame I plead the blood of Jesus Christ. Taking that sacrifice into my hands, as it were, and going into the Holiest of all, presenting it as the basis of my forgiveness, immediately I am forgiven and cleansed. I have peace and rest and deliverance from the guilt and penalty of that sin—immediately. But the consequences remain. When Nathan spoke to David by parable and said to him, "David, Thou art the man," David's silence was ended, his heart was broken, and he cried, "I have sinned!" Immediately the answer came, "The Lord hath put away thy sin, but the sword shall never depart from thy house" (see 2 Samuel 12:7-13). So far as the sin lay between David's soul and God, it was removed immediately by his confession. But so far as the consequences were concerned, they followed him for years. Bathsheba's son died. His son Amnon was murdered. Absalom betrayed him. The kingdom was torn in two. All of this was the discipline of the government of God from which there was no escape. It was the harvest which he had sown.

This truth needs no further underlining. Recall the assurance in Isaiah 40:1 when God said, "Speak ye comfortably to Jerusalem, and cry unto her, that her warfare is accomplished, that her iniquity is pardoned:" and compare that with the language of chapter 54, which speaks of her ruin and waste.

I want to say to you with deep conviction, yet with great love in my heart, that through repentance and faith we receive the immediate and perfect pardon of Jesus, but if the ruin of Jerusalem says anything at all to me, it reminds me of the scar that sin has left. It reminds me of the lost years and the wasted opportunities, and the Word of God comes with deep penetration, saying, "O barren, thou that didst not bear, thou that didst not travail." To serve the Lord without result, to have little sense of His presence in your life, to suffer intolerably in your mind, all of these are the disciplines of the government of God. The natural consequences of sin remain long after the penalty and guilt have been removed and buried in the deepest sea. One look of confession and faith and we are forgiven, but we sow what we reap, and we reap what we have sown.

Would you please put yourself in that picture, and ask yourself this question in the presence of God: Can it be that there is any connection between that and your fruitless service, and perhaps the lack of evidence of God working in your church?

This is not the only side of the picture, however, for in His mercy God also speaks concerning *the discovery of the grace of God.*

Notice that He speaks to this barren, fruitless, desolate city and says, "Sing . . . break forth into singing, and cry aloud."

"But, Lord, how can I sing? With the city in ruins, with the temple burned, with the marks and scars and fruitlessness, how can I sing?"

Sing, says the Lord, not because of what you are, but because of something I have promised you: "Enlarge the place of thy tent, and let them stretch forth the curtains of thine habitations: spare not, lengthen thy cords, and strengthen thy stakes; For thou shalt break forth on the right hand and on the left. . . . Fear not; for thou shalt not be ashamed: neither be thou confounded; for thou shalt not be put to shame. . . . For thy Maker is thine husband; the Lord of hosts is his name; and thy Redeemer the Holy One of Israel; the God of the whole earth shall he be called" (vs. 2-5).

Here the Lord is saying to His people who are conscious of barrenness, "Sing! Prepare for the incoming of a great host, and make room for a great ingathering and a great harvest!"

"But, Lord, You told me that though You forgive me, the result of my backsliding must stay with me. You cannot give me back those years of bondage. You cannot remove the scar, and you cannot prevent the inevitable recoil of what I have been. Lord, how can I sing?"

Yes, the Lord replies, you can sing! You will sing as you did when you came out of Egypt, only with this difference—you will not be so exuberant as you used to be. But in your heart there will be a deep insight into the grace of God which, in addition to giving you an abundant pardon, can transform the past, can change the brier into a myrtle and the thorn into a fir tree, and can make fruitlessness become fruitfulness. Yes, you will yet sing.

Thank God, He can make men and women in middle life sing again with a joy that has been chastened by a memory of their past failures. Adam's sin was overruled to the blessing of the world, and so in His goodness you and I may rise out of the fall, triumph instead of sensing defeat, and through years in a wilderness we may enter into the land of blessing and victory.

The captivity of God's people was disastrous as it brought suffering and loss for a period of years. They were never the same again, yet in the overruling mercy of God, how He blessed them. In the lessons of those years of captivity they learned three things: First, the Holy One of Israel is the God of all the earth (v. 5). Second, they began to understand the meaning of worship, and to realize that it did not require the temple, the altar, the sacrifice. It was out of the days and years of captivity there was born the synagogue with its simple form of worship, with the approach of each individual soul to God. Third, they were faced with a world mission. They were given to understand they were stewards of God's truth (v. 3). The chastisement of God was the means of touching the darkness of all that affliction and transforming it into pure gold for His glory.

The man who bears the scars of the past is made intent on the saving of others who are the victims of that which used to wound and bind him. There is no one with such a burden for the man who is gripped by some habit as one who has been delivered from that very thing, who is back to face his colleagues with a passion for them that he knew nothing about until the Lord brought about his own recovery, and lifted him up out of the mess of his life. The father who has failed in his home responsibilities has become strangely tender in his love. Into the man who has suffered from the results of his own sin, even as a Christian, God has put the soul of a prophet, the burden of the intercessor to pray with humility, tenderness, and understanding of the temptations of other people. The prodigal who has been pardoned can speak of the Father's love in a way that the elder brother never could.

We may, therefore, bitterly lament the loss to ourselves and others caused by our sinfulness, yet we sing with a new meaning as we see God beginning to transform the waste and restoring to us the years. As a result of this there are new thoughts of Him, there is a new sense of intimacy in our fellowship with Him, there is a new passion that takes in the whole world in its need of Christ.

Finally, see *the deliverance of the chastisement of God.* There is a world of difference between chastisement and punishment. Punishment is for the Saviour who bore the guilt and penalty of our sin upon the cross; chastisement is for every child of God who is made one with Jesus by faith. If the past with all its failures sometimes recoils and hits back at you, and there seems to be no escape from it, don't say that is punishment. It is chastisement that we might escape the condemnation of the world, that we might profit by correction. We are chastised in order that the Lord might make us tender and usable.

I would put in this word of warning: Beware of allowing the chastening hand of our loving Father to alienate you from Him, but rather let it cause you to lie down and rest in Him, knowing that whom the Lord loves He chasteneth. I would rather be chastened for my sin now than meet God at the judgment seat concerning it. It was David who cried, ". . . let me fall now into the hand of the Lord; for very great are his mercies: but let me not fall into the hand of man" (1 Chronicles 21:13).

Notice the wonderful language of Isaiah 54:10, "For the mountains shall depart, and the hills be removed; but my kindness shall not depart from thee, neither shall the covenant of my peace be removed, saith the Lord that hath mercy on thee."

He has entered into a covenant with us that is going to outlast every mountain and hill. Perhaps we have been careless and apathetic and cold, and brought suffering to others and to ourselves, but God has used the consequences of that as a furnace to consume our sin and drive us to the wounded side of the Lord Jesus. Throughout all our times of waywardness He has followed us to lead us back to Himself, and through all our wanderings He accomplishes His purpose in us of holiness and purity of heart. For ". . . no chastening for the present seemeth to be joyous, but grievous: nevertheless afterward it yieldeth the peaceable fruit of righteousness unto them which are exercised thereby" (Hebrews 12:11).

Many people make their circumstances an excuse for a life of real consecration and service. They complain that the cares and troubles of life hinder them from living a clear-cut testimony to the saving and keeping power of the Lord Jesus. It is true that many of God's children live under most trying circumstances and with exceptional cares and troubles, but it could be that these particular trials come from God as His messenger of love. Calamity and heartbreak can prove to be His call to come away from the world to trust implicitly in Him. These things may be sent from Him in order that the Christian may prove His strength.

If this is the case, then we know He has allowed these things, and we can welcome them from Him. Our first care is to glorify

Him in the circumstance, whatever it may be, and trust Him to make it a blessing, for He has no purpose toward His children than that of infinite love.

If you are going through this particular testing at this time, accept it, look to Jesus to bring the comfort of His sympathy, the courage of His victory, and the consciousness of His strength. Submission to His will, even in trial, unlocks the door to a fruitful life, for learning the lessons of chastening is basic to the formation of Christian character.

Chastening is also a mark of sonship. In family life, discipline is a part of education. In the will of God, and in the very nature of things, sin and suffering go together, and love will cause suffering for the greater good of casting out the sin. It is essential for the Christian to learn that suffering in the will of God is the chastening of love. If you doubt this, look away to Jesus, the Son of God's love, the Man of Sorrows, the Prince of Sufferers. How close in Him is the relation between suffering and love, suffering and victory over sin, suffering and perfection of character, suffering and glory. He was indeed made perfect through suffering, and all the glory and loveliness of His character was all the outcome of His willingness to drink the last dregs of the cup of sorrow. By draining it empty He became the mighty conqueror of sin, and now He breathes His strength into His obedient people.

Finally, chastening prepares God's people for eternity, for suffering is His messenger to lead us into fitness for His presence. In Hebrews 12:11 it says, ". . . for the present . . . nevertheless afterward." Here is eternity thrown into the scale; here is the reckoning of faith and not of sense. This is what Christ did, ". . . who for the joy that was set before him endured the cross" (Hebrews 12:2).

When the storm sweeps the ocean into mountainous waves, it is all quiet down in the depths, for the storm is only on the surface. Even so, "the present" is swallowed up in the "afterward"—the light affliction is but for a moment and works for us an eternal weight of glory. The storm may be on the circumference, but peace may reign in the soul. So take courage, get your eyes afresh on the Saviour, and learn deeply the lessons that lead to a life of fruitfulness in service and testimony, and fellowship with Him.

13

Isaiah 54:11-17

The Wealth of the Christian

No weapon that is formed against thee shall prosper; and every tongue that shall rise against thee in judgment thou shalt condemn. This is the heritage of the servants of the Lord, and their righteousness is of me, saith the Lord.

Isaiah 54:17

In the previous study we were considering the first part of this chapter of God's Word, especially in reference to verse 8 and its setting. The picture was of a people who were suffering the chastisement of God for their sins, and because of this they were tasting the bitter outcome of fruitlessness in service. We recognize that, though through the blood of Jesus Christ the penalty and the guilt of sin are immediately dealt with and "buried in the deepest sea" (*see* Micah 7:19), yet very often the consequences of a man's sin follow him for the rest of his life here. But in all of this we saw the Lord even overruling the consequences to His glory, and making a people through chastisement to become spiritually enriched.

Now here is another picture. God is speaking to a people who refuse to be comforted: "O thou afflicted, tossed with tempest, and not comforted, behold, I will lay thy stones with fair colours, and lay thy foundations with sapphires" (v. 11). So conscious are they of their shame and guilt that nothing God could say could reassure them.

How often that is the case with His people today. Satan trips them up, puts them down, and then tells them that it is hopeless to begin again: they might as well give up. Have you heard that voice? I am sure you have, and in that mood nothing that any preacher or friend can say, or even the Word of God itself, seems to penetrate.

Yet look at the language of our text: "No weapon that is formed against thee shall prosper; and every tongue that shall rise against thee in judgment thou shalt condemn. This is the heritage of the servants of the Lord, and their righteousness is of me, saith the Lord" (v. 17). Please observe that this is said to exactly the same people who, in the first verse of this chapter, have been faced with the barrenness and fruitlessness of their lives. But God is telling them now of a beauty and loveliness that is to be all their own, and which is going to emerge on the very scene of their disaster and shame.

Now I am well aware that the primary reference of this passage of Scripture is to the rebuilding of Jerusalem which was effected under the leadership of Nehemiah. But there is an infinitely deeper and fuller meaning to our text than that, for from the wreckage of sin, from the ruin of the Fall, and from the rubble and rubbish of every human effort to build civilization without God, there is emerging a people who have been redeemed by the blood of the cross, and who are indwelt by the Holy Spirit of God. Such people are called the body of Christ, the church.

". . . more are the children of the desolate [that is the Gentile] than the children of the married wife [that is the Jew], saith the Lord" (v. 1). ". . . thy seed shall inherit the Gentiles, and make the desolate cities to be inhabited" (v. 3). This is that of which Paul speaks in his letter to the Colossians, when he tells of "the mystery which has been hid from past generations but now is made manifest to His saints, to whom God would make known what is the riches of the glory of His mystery, which is Christ in you, the hope of glory" (*see* Colossians 1:26).

Here then, emerging from all the wreck of society and the tragedy of human history without God, is a people (and I pray that each one of us is among that people) redeemed by the blood of Christ, made partakers of His nature. Each one is being watched by the eye of the One who is the architect of the soul, God Himself, our Father. The life of each believer has been wrought upon by hands that are unseen, and he is being tested constantly by the application of the truth of God's Word and the righteousness that God demands of those who have been redeemed.

The Lord is constantly putting before us the plummet, the line of test, until one day when Jesus comes with His own—blessed day!—there will be fulfilled the vision of Revelation 21:2-4, "And I . . . saw the holy city, new Jerusalem, coming down from God out of heaven, prepared as a bride adorned for her husband. And I heard a great voice out of heaven saying, Behold, the tabernacle of God is with men, and he will dwell with them, and they shall be his people, and God himself shall be with them, and be their God. And God shall wipe away all tears from their eyes; and there shall be no more death, neither sorrow, nor crying, neither shall there be any more pain: for the former things are passed away."

This is the ultimate of everything in history. That is the only thing that makes sense, and the person who fails to keep his eyes on the goal will be utterly confused in days like these. The only thing that will keep him sane as a Christian is to keep his mind on God's ultimate purposes, and set his heart to achieve them, as his eyes are fixed on the Lord Jesus, his Saviour.

Here in this chapter is the picture of the city being built and in the course of construction. Or, to change the metaphor, the bride in the course of preparation. To put it in simple, plain language, here is the picture of your life and the school of which God is the Principal. The world is your classroom, life's problems and battles, tests and trials, are the members of the faculty, and you are one of the students. Oh, let us not hesitate to appropriate this portion of Scripture to ourselves, for the chapter closes with this word, "This is the heritage of the servants of the Lord." So I can nestle in here and find comfort to my heart.

Keeping before us, therefore, the picture of the building (one that is often used in the New Testament, as in Ephesians 2:22), let us see the pricelessness of this building, which has to do with our worship; then the privilege of the inhabitants of the building, which has to do with our witness; and finally the protection of the inhabitants of the building, which has to do with our warfare.

In studying any passage of Scripture, the first question should be, "What has God to say to me in these verses?" This is what we are seeking now, and I want to speak to you as those who are members of the body of Christ. Maybe some of you are not, but you may become so immediately by receiving Jesus Christ into your life as your personal Lord and Sovereign. In confession of your sin and repentance thereof, you may turn to God and become His child—born again, a member of the body and family of Jesus Christ.

First consider *the pricelessness of the building*, which has to do with our worship. See some of the stones which God produces when He manufactures a saint. There are three of them in verses 11 and 12: "I will lay thy stones with fair colours, and lay thy foundations with sapphires. And I will make thy windows of agates, and thy gates of carbuncles, and all thy borders of pleasant stones."

Sapphires, agates, carbuncles—what are they? Jewels? Yes, but what is a jewel? By nature a jewel is simply a lump of stone, dull material, possibly some form of clay. Where then lies the difference between the beauty of a jewel and a bit of ordinary stone or clay? Just this: the beauty and value of a jewel is due to a process which is called crystallization that has been conducted under exceptional circumstances, under immense pressure and in intense heat, probably over a period of centuries. A jewel is no more than a bit of ordinary clay which has passed through an extraordinary experience.

Now here is God showing something of what He is after in our lives, something of the beauty that He has in mind to produce, the quality of material He designs for His people. Ours is a fiery baptism. Ours are the heat and pressure, and we count them hard. We complain and grumble and cry, and even give up. But look what God is producing! Sapphires for foundations, agates for windows, and I think the word is better rendered "pearls" for gates.

A foundation of sapphire, one of the more precious of all jewels, it is blue in color, and reminds us of the clear sky and deep ocean. You often find this analogy in Scripture, as in Exodus 24:10 when the elders of Israel saw a pavement of sapphire under the feet of the God of Israel. In Exodus 28:18 it is one of

the precious stones on the breastplate of judgment. And in
Ezekiel 1:26, in his vision the throne of God was as the appearance of a sapphire, bright, brilliant, clear blue. In John's vision
of the new Jerusalem in Revelation 21, the foundations of the
city were garnished with all manner of precious stones, and the
second among them was the sapphire. Blue and gold were
predominant among the colorings of the tabernacle, and I think
I would be right in saying that the gold speaks of the glory and
majesty of God, while the blue tells of His love.

Underneath the life of every Christian, undergirding it, out
of sight and deep down below everything, if you dig down as
far as you can, you will come at last to bedrock, and what will
you find there?

> We have an anchor that keeps the soul
>   Steadfast and sure while the billows roll,
> Fastened to the Rock which cannot move,
>   Grounded firm and deep in the Saviour's love.

I tell you, as enduring and as eternal as the throne of God, the
great fact which underpins every child of God—the blood of the
cross, the eternal purpose of His redemption that His grace
should triumph where sin did once abound—is the love of God.
Whatever, therefore, may be the circumstances that are affect-
ing you right now, at this moment, deep down at bedrock, there
is the sapphire quality of the love of God.

"Windows of agates," a jewel which bears upon it the mark
of fire. An agate is not a transparent jewel like a clear-cut crys-
tal, nor is it opaque like a piece of brick or flint, but it is partially
transparent, admitting the light's rays. God says concerning His
children that He will make windows of agates. In other words,
He takes the affliction, the battle, the problem, and makes it a
window through which you see Him. Now that vision will always be partially obscure in this life. We shall always see
through a glass darkly, or as J.B. Phillips renders it in his *Letters
to Young Churches*, "All we see [now] is the baffling reflection
of reality." We are like people who are looking at a great land-
scape through a small mirror. We shall not know as we are
known in this life, yet there are these wonderful windows. And

the one who is, in verse 11, "afflicted, tossed with tempest, and not comforted," is the one who will learn to praise God for all of this, because through the fire God has admitted some light. He is laying in your life the foundation of sapphires, His love. He is putting into your life the windows of agate through which you can see and understand something of the meaning of what He is doing with you.

"Gates of pearl"—all twelve gates of the city of Jerusalem in Revelation 21 are of pearl. And just what is a pearl? It is the direct result of an injury that has been done to the life that produced it. You all know that a pearl is found in the shell of an oyster, but how does it come to be there? A grain of sand or some other substance has entered under the shell, and immediately it is covered with layer upon layer of mother-of-pearl until at last the thing which has caused the injury is transformed into a beautiful and valuable pearl. You see, the pearl has become the answer of the life which was injured to the thing that injured it. The pearl began by hurting, but the answer of the oyster it hurt was to take hold of that grain of sand and transform it into an object of matchless beauty and worth.

In Matthew 13:45 and 46 is the parable of the pearl of great price. Of all the parables which Jesus told there is none which has suffered from such bad interpretation as this one. The pearl of great price is not Jesus Christ, in spite of what some hymns say. You do not buy salvation; you receive it as God's gift. What then is the pearl of great price? There is to be gathered out of the sin, evil, and confusion of these days a most glorious jewel for the possession of God, the church of Jesus Christ, and with this in His mind the Master goes away and sells all that He has in order to purchase it. He did not go away from earth to heaven; He came from heaven to earth. One day we came to Him in our sin, and in our coming to Him He was injured, wounded, bruised, and slain. But the answer of the life that was injured and hurt to those who wounded Him was to make over to us His loveliness and thus produce a pearl. Every pearl of beauty is a reminder that there has been a stab of pain. Every fragrant Christian life, the gates of which are of pearl, is only so because of the wounds which once that life inflicted upon Him when God was denied, refused, and rejected. His answer to our hurting Him is to make us a pearl of great price.

May I apply that in a subjective sense? There is no gate which leads to the abundant life which does not cost. There is no display of the grace of God in a man's life that has not been preceded by a personal crucifixion of the flesh. I would ask this question lovingly: What is your answer to the friend who has injured you? What is your response when you are hurt and wounded? Is it to say, "I'll fight him to the last"? If so, then I suggest you are not a Christian. Or is it to say, "Lord, I am sure that brother (or sister) is wrong, but You see how he has hurt me. But dear Lord, by Thy grace I am not going to fight back. Help me to love him, and to restore fellowship with him." The answer to the life that has been hurt is to be the means in the hand of God of transforming the life that hurt, thus producing a pearl.

Such is the pricelessness of our building, which is worship.

Now see *the privileges of the inhabitants of the building,* which is our witness. "And all thy children shall be taught of the Lord; and great shall be the peace of thy children" (v. 13).

In John 6:45 the Lord quotes this verse, "It is written in the prophets, And they shall be all taught of God. Every man therefore that hath heard, and hath learned of the Father, cometh unto me."

Going back to the metaphor of the school, He is the Principal: He regulates the curriculum, He delegates to nobody else the task of educating His children. But how often we hear but do not learn!

In a child's school report recently, among other good things in the report was this statement, "Attention often wanders to other things which have nothing to do with the subject, and so the lesson is returned to be done again." As I go back in the pages of memory that has a somewhat familiar ring! How often as I sat in a classroom I was thinking about the football field, or anything on earth but what the man was trying to teach me. I heard him, but I did not learn. In the school of God how often I hear but fail to learn. If we did learn we would come to the feet of Jesus, and great would be our peace. Instead we are restless, frustrated, unhappy, defeated, just because we hear but do not learn.

What lesson has the Lord been trying to teach you recently? Could it be the lesson of true repentance and forsaking of sin? Could it be the necessity of obedience to His Word? Could it be the need to trust Him, resting in His promise, and leaving your situation in His hands? But you will not learn. You still disobey, you still sin, you still try to fight the battle yourself. Yet the Scripture says, "Great peace have they which love thy law" (Psalm 119:165).

How powerful such a testimony is for Jesus, but how ineffective and damaging it is when I hear but I do not learn! We profess faith for many years, and yet spiritually we are still in infancy. We fail to grow up, and reveal it by our attitudes, our reactions, and our fighting.

The Bible says that the privilege of God's people is that they shall be all taught of God. Don't you think that is the mark of those who are clearly His, the dividing line between the true and the false today? The false hear, but do not learn. The true hear and learn. In the parable of the sower there is the seed by the wayside, that on stony ground, seed among thorns, and seed on good ground. All of them were those who heard the Word, but only those who learned are called the seed which fell on good ground. Are you a hearer only, or does it make any difference to you what you hear?

Such is the privilege of the inhabitants of the city: they shall be all taught of God.

Thirdly, *the protection of the inhabitants of the city*, which is our warfare: "No weapon that is formed against thee shall prosper; and every tongue that shall rise against thee in judgment thou shalt condemn" (v. 17). Many are the weapons that are formed against the Christian. Many are the tongues which speak falsely against the man of God. See the last part of verse 16, "I have created the waster to destroy." The first part of the verse says, "I have created the smith that bloweth the coals in the fire"—the emphasis is that the Lord creates these powers. In other words, don't be afraid when you see the pressure coming. Don't be afraid when you see something blowing up the fire and producing an instrument of destruction. God has made even that instrument, and it can do no more than God permits, for no weapon formed against you shall prosper, and every tongue that is raised against you in judgment you shall condemn.

You cannot escape the ordeal of which I am speaking. The Lord Jesus warned us that "in the world you shall have tribulation" (John 16:33). "If they have hated and persecuted Me, they will do the same to you. The servant is not above his Master." But I want to say that nothing on earth can ever hurt the child of God. Our responsibility in every situation, I believe, is to do what is right in His sight, with a single eye to His glory, with a concern for His will, and to be regardless of the opinions of anyone else. Live above the strife of tongues, the deceit, the sharp practices of other people. Never vindicate yourself, never take revenge. God will turn the edge of every weapon that is formed against you back on the person who uses it, and He will silence every whispering, accusing voice. That is your heritage, if you are His child. Your honor is in the keeping of the Lord Himself. Therefore do not lower yourself to the mean, despicable level of some professing Christians whose backbiting and bitterness are evidences of their true character. Leave your case in His hands and watch Him work.

As fellow travelers along the pilgrim road to glory, remember the pricelessness of the structure. Keep the goal in view, to be a jewel in His crown.

Remember the privileges of every inhabitant of the city, that they shall all be taught of God, and be sure that you are a student in His school, hearing and learning from Him.

Rejoice in the protection of every inhabitant of the city and keep your eyes on the risen Lord Jesus. Let Him fight for you, for victory in Him is assured.